ORDINARY HEROES

When the Walls of Life are Crumbling

DAVID WALLS

ACCENT BOOKS
Denver, Colorado

ACCENT BOOKS

A division of Accent Publications
12100 West Sixth Avenue
P.O. Box 15337
Denver, CO 80215

Library of Congress Catalog Number 90-85033

ISBN 0-89636-271-X

To Patricia,

My wife, my best friend, my HERO!
You are the "wind beneath my wings..."
an ordinary hero...with extraordinary gifts.

Thank you!

CONTENTS

FOREWORD

It is no small accomplishment to present time-honored truth in a fresh way. But this is what David R. Walls accomplishes with distinction in *Ordinary Heroes*.

With an energetic style which is lucid and electric, Dr. Walls takes us into the heart of ancient Nehemiah, the peerless leader, and shows us that ordinary people can become spiritual heroes midst daunting circumstances. Serious Christians will find much here to help them stand tall against the opposition, criticism and alienation which surround a committed life.

There are no cliche bromides here, but rather rigorous Biblical truth presented with eyes wide open to contemporary life. Dave Walls is a reader—and we find fresh insights quarried not only from the great writings of the past, but also from present voices as diverse as Chuck Swindoll and Christopher Lasch, and A.W. Tozer.

Ordinary Heroes is eminently practical and "user friendly" —the kind of book which will be passed along from friend to friend.

It is a pleasure to commend this fine work.

R. Kent Hughes
Wheaton, Illinois

Princeton sociologist, Suzanne Keller worries that too many of today's heroes are media creations. In response to the Roper survey she wrote:

These people are tapped (as heroes) because they're always featured in the media, especially movies and T.V. I'm not sure the celebrities are heroes. With many, you could ask, 'What moral position have they taken in life? What risk have they taken?' (These heroes) are idols of consumption—(people) who entertain or divert you. [1]

. . .BUT THEY DO NOT LEAD US. Almost completely absent from this list of heroes and heroines are *leaders* from any sphere of life. Perhaps our young people are simply reflecting to us what *TIME* magazine observed in their Nov. 9, 1987 cover story. The article was captioned, "Who's in Charge? The Nation Calls for Leadership and There is No One Home."

The clear need of our day is for *proper leadership*, ordinary people who are willing to stand up and make a difference. Before you say, "That isn't me. I'm not a leader," read a bit further.

Over 20 years ago, John Gardner, in the Annual Report of the Carnegie Corporation, expressed the value of leadership then and now.

Leaders have a significant role in creating the state of mind that is the society. They can serve as symbols of the moral unity of the society. They can express the values that hold the society together. Most important they can conceive and articulate goals that lift people out of petty preoccupations, carry them above the conflicts that tear a society apart, and unite them in the pursuit of objectives worthy of their best efforts. [2]

Isn't that what God calls every Christian to do?

It is that kind of leadership that oozes from the pores of a man, whose life has long since been covered with the dust of time, but whose influence and model ought never to be forgotten. The chances are good that you haven't spent a major part of your week thinking about him. This man lived in the Far East some 450 years or so before the birth of Christ. His name was Nehemiah and an entire book of the Old Testament bears his name and tells his story. There is no portion of the Old Testament that provides us with a better model of *dedicated, discerning leadership* than the book of Nehemiah.

He is a man for our generation. And whether on the assembly line or in the corporate office, in an educational sphere of influence or in the management of your home or church. . . Nehemiah echoes across the canyon of history and invades our present-day life with a message of clarity and reality.

In order to understand that message, we need to drop briefly into the cylinder of time and consider *Nehemiah's place and position.* They are outlined for us in the opening sentences of his story, as recorded in Nehemiah 1:1-2.

The words of Nehemiah. . .in the month of Chislev in the twentieth year, while I was in Susa the capital, that Hanani, one of my brothers, and some men from Judah came; and I asked them concerning the Jews who had escaped and had survived the captivity, and about Jerusalem.

About 150 years before Nehemiah's day, Israel as a nation, centered in Jerusalem, had been invaded and completely defeated by the armies of ancient Babylon. Israel became a captive nation. The bulk of her population were dragged from their homes and led 800 miles east. . .to the country of Babylon . . .a place in today's world on the Iran-Iraq border in the Persian Gulf. Left behind to pick up the pieces were the incompetents— those who were physically handicapped by age or deformity. In the course of time, the government changed hands, from the Babylonians to the Persians, but the Jews remained captives.

Into that captivity Nehemiah was born and raised. But he is

11

drowning in a sea of selfishness and discontent.

Nehemiah didn't feel that way. His values, his security, did not rest in his career or his possessions. They rested in his relationship with his God because, as we'll see in a moment, Nehemiah walked away from it all. He vacated his plush office downtown, turned his keys in, and cut up his gold American Express card. He traded a cosmopolitan and modern city for a pile of rubble in the shell of a city called Jerusalem.

Why would he do that? Why turn your back on a sure thing? Because he was *leader* material. Real leader material. Nehemiah's principles were cemented in his relationship with God. Even a pagan ruler knew he could be trusted. His character, his integrity, were Rock-solid. He had been faithful in the smallest, most boring tasks as well as on the front-line of danger. I sense that even in verses 2 and 3 of the story, where we find him presented with *a problem*.

> *...Hanani, one of my brothers, and some men from Judah came; and I asked them concerning the Jews who had escaped and had survived the captivity, and about Jerusalem. And they said to me, "The remnant there in the province who survived the captivity are in great distress and reproach, and the wall of Jerusalem is broken down and its gates are burned with fire."*

Unexpectedly, Nehemiah's brother arrives in town. Apparently, he had moved back to Jerusalem as the government loosened its immigration laws. But now he's back in Persia and Nehemiah asks how things are going. The verb "ask" means "to inquire, to consult." In other words, this was more than a passing interest that prompted his questions. Nehemiah was genuinely interested in the city and the people, and he is the one who did the inquiring.

People of genuine integrity make it a habit to ask about *the welfare of others*. You'll note that Nehemiah didn't use this as an opportunity to hand out his latest resume or public relations portfolio. Good leaders ask about others before they think of selling themselves. They don't wait for rumors to circulate or reports to filter down. They initiate sincere concern for people.

Do you? Do you notice when people you work with are absent? Having trouble? Do you pay attention to those in your church family who seem to have dropped out? Do you call them or drop by personally to find out what is wrong? Do you notice the joys and sorrows in your own family? Are you sensitive to what's going on in the life of your teenager? Do your wife's eyes. . .your husband's sighs. . .tell you anything? Do you pursue those intuitive, yet painful observations? Ordinary heroes care about other *people*. They reflect a Christlike concern. And they expect honest answers. The response that Nehemiah received was brutally honest.

His brother could have just as easily have answered: "Jerusalem. . .hey, I've got to tell you, things couldn't be better, Nehemiah. I mean, with our urban development scheme, and the long-range economic forecasting, why, it's better than it ever was. Everything's great."

That's often how we answer, isn't it? Now, I'm not talking about dumping your load on a stranger. But, when a friend slides by and asks those kinds of questions, how honest are we? About our marriage, our family life, our job, our emotions?

Hanani was honest. The answer Nehemiah received was full of hurt. The people were in "great trouble" the text says. The word means "misery." For the last 150 years they had been beaten down. In fact, very recently apparently, the Jews who were there had tried to start rebuilding the city. But their enemies had forced them to stop and destroyed virtually all that they had worked on. Without a city wall to protect them, the people were defenseless and were constantly being harassed.

More than that, verse 3 says they endured "disgrace" or "reproach." The idea is that of bearing the brunt of cutting words. The Jews were being criticized and slandered by people who were enemies of God. Put it all together and you have no hope, only lives filled with despair.

The news from home wasn't very good, and it may be equally dismal in your world—although you might not admit it. You may feel severe distress about an upcoming doctor's appointment. Despair from a demanding schedule. Loneliness aggravated by a best friend's recent relocation. Financial pressures may be coloring your world dark gray. Others feel no hope since being rejected by a spouse or alienated by associates at the office.

Even normal parenting responsibilities can produce this kind of stress. Did you know that 1 in 7 parents have a child with learning disabilities? One in 8 have a child with mental or emotional problems. One in 10 have a child who has been threatened or hurt by a stranger. About 1 in 10 admits having a child who uses drugs or has a drinking problem, and the same number of parents have been confronted by the problem of a pregnant teenager.[5] The news from our homes isn't very good today.

When the walls in our lives are crumbling. . .we understand the problem in Jerusalem.

The following is a letter, written by someone we'll never meet, but who, perhaps, writes for some of us.

> *...I am writing you from this motel because I have run away from my loving husband, my six-year-old daughter (Annie) and my five-month-old son (Paulie). My little girl is a beautiful blonde with blue eyes, but she throws temper tantrums and irritates me to the breaking point. My son seems to cry twenty-four hours a day. I need one uninterrupted night's sleep so badly.*
>
> *I've tried so hard to be a good mother and wife. . . .I've*

16

wanted to meet my responsibilities to my family, but I'm completely exhausted. I became a monster this past week. I hit my daughter across the face, bruised her arm from shaking her so hard, yelled and screamed and cried, and then wanted to die from guilt.

I've come here to try to get a hold of what's left of me, but I don't think I can. I feel my prayers take too long to be answered, or else I don't recognize the answers when they come. When I'm home, there's not enough time to even brush my teeth, let alone pray about Annie's behavior and my inferiority as a parent. . . .

We spent (a lot of) money last month to take four counseling sessions on parenting techniques. Well, some of it works but some of it is too far removed from my child's misbehavior to do any good. Annie was hostile and aggressive even before Paulie arrived. I can't help wanting to get away from her. She spent a week with Grandma and went to Disneyland recently. I really felt guilty because I hardly missed her.

I just talked with my husband by telephone and he said Annie was having a temper tantrum. She wants to go find me and I don't even want to go home! I adore my husband. I've had little chance to show him how much, and I've been blessed with a daughter and son, both of whom I always wanted to have. The problem now is that I can't handle the ROUTINE PANIC of our lives. Next Thursday will be my twenty-eighth birthday. Please help me!" [6]

How might you respond to that kind of pain? Notice the way Nehemiah did. . . .It's detailed in verse 4 of his story:

Now it came about when I heard these words, I sat down and wept and mourned for days; and I was fasting and praying before the God of heaven.

Nehemiah was a long way from the problem, in both time and distance. "Out of sight and out of mind," could have been his attitude, or "it's not my problem." But he didn't say that. . . because his heart responded to the needs of people—even people he didn't know. He even includes himself in their errors, their sins. Listen to the way he prays.

Let Thine ear now be attentive and thine eyes open to hear the prayer of Thy servant which I am praying before Thee now, day and night, on behalf of the sons of Israel Thy servants, confessing the sins of the sons of Israel which we have sinned against Thee; I and my father's house have sinned. We have acted very corruptly against Thee and have not kept the commandments, nor the statutes, nor the ordinances which Thou didst command Thy servant Moses (1:6-7).

Part of the reason why God allowed Israel to go into captivity 150 years earlier was because of their disregard for Him—their constant sin. Nehemiah wasn't even thought of back then, let alone involved. Yet, out of a heart of compassion, he includes himself.

Have you ever done that? Have you ever shared the blame, taken the heat, or been punished for the wrong. . .*when you weren't involved*? Perhaps you did so out of love for a friend. Ordinary heroes often do that. They take the heat for what isn't their fault. That's Nehemiah. No plea bargaining. No excuses. No rationalizations or blame shifting. Instead, he took the heat.

Consider something else about Nehemiah's response. He did not pretend that the problems weren't there. He *dealt with reality.* Some people think the best way to handle problems is to pretend there aren't any. That is especially true in marriage. Just close your eyes and ignore it, and it will go away. Not a chance! Nehemiah understood that integrity and honesty don't ignore problems.

But now, what is so stunning about this is his level of emotion. *The man sat down and cried* over the situation! The verb "wept" in verse 4 suggests that he was in so much grief that he, at times, literally wailed in agony over the hurts of his people. When is the last time you wept about another person's problems?

Most of us are so preoccupied with ourselves, with our needs, with our inconveniences that we don't take the time to identify with those of others...and so we rarely weep for them. But those with a godly heart of compassion cry, too. Maybe not out in the open for all to see, but they cry. Do you?

Somehow, men think that we must be strong and always in control. Crying seems to say that we are weak and out of control. However, if we were to ask our wives about this, most would tell us that she would willingly die to see a moment of weakness, a hint of frailty, the essence of vulnerability. She would welcome that with compassion and love. Yet, we continue on our stonefaced way. We men have been taught that approach to life since we were kids. Some of us actually pride ourselves on the fact that no one has ever seen us cry. But why is that a source of pride? Jesus Christ was a man of tears. Jeremiah was dubbed the weeping prophet. Tears are not a sign of weakness, and people who are willing to be Christlike are not afraid to admit that, because they cry too. There is a circle of family and friends before whom they are willing to be transparent, honest, and vulnerable.

One of my favorite writers, Max Lucado, reveals the depth of care in our tears as he weaves these thoughts together for us in his book, *No Wonder They Call Him The Savior*.

Tears. Those tiny drops of humanity. Those round, wet balls of fluid that tumble from our eyes, creep down our cheeks, and splash on the floor of our hearts. . . . They are miniature messengers; on call 24 hours a day to substitute for crippled words. They drip, drop, and pour from the corner of our souls, carrying with them the deepest emotions we possess. They tumble down our faces with announcements that range from the most blissful joy to darkest despair.

The principle is simple: WHEN WORDS ARE MOST EMPTY, TEARS ARE MOST APT.

A tearstain on a letter says much more than the sum of all its words. A tear falling on a casket says what a spoken farewell never could. What summons a mother's compassion and concern more quickly than a tear on a child's cheek? What gives more support than a sympathetic tear on the face of a friend?

Tears. . .those tiny drops of humanity. [7]

We tolerate stresses and pressures more easily if at least one other person knows we are enduring it. In fact, if more Christians made themselves available to help and to listen to others when the troubles in life first start, there would be far fewer numbers of us having to go for professional help. Caring Christians contribute to the mental and emotional health of their fellow church members, friends, and family. It is those who care in the ordinary stresses of life who are heroes in God's sight.

That is where we find Nehemiah. On the cutting edge of pain. Nehemiah's first lesson for us is: *You never lighten the load for others unless, first, you have felt with them the pressure in your own soul.* You are never used of God to bring blessing until God has opened your eyes and made you see things as they really are.

Nehemiah saw things as they were and he wept. That is his initial response. But there is something more. *He prayed and he planned.*

*I sat down and wept and mourned for days; and I was
fasting and praying before the God of heaven. And I said,
"I beseech Thee, O Lord God of heaven, the great and
awesome God, who preserves the covenant and lovingkindness for those who love Him and keep His commandments. . . .O Lord, I beseech Thee, may thine ear be
attentive to the prayer of Thy servant and the prayer of
Thy servants who delight to revere Thy name, and make
Thy servant successful today, and grant him compassion
before this man" (verses 1:4b-5,11).*

Too often we give lip service to the necessity of prayer, then
we go on as if *we* can meet our own needs.

Nehemiah didn't hang a crystal on his rearview mirror. . . .He
didn't walk across a bed of hot coals. . . .He turned his attention
in prayer to God. That's what the ordinary heroes of life do, too.

When was the last time you prayed about a business decision? A family or marital crisis? A friend? When was the last
time you prayed about anything? Not just any quickie prayer
like, "Now I lay me down to sleep. . . ." Look at Nehemiah's
prayer.

It begins with thoughts about God. It then moves on to
confession of sin and *only* then does it focus on a specific
request. When Nehemiah prayed, he stood in reverential awe of
the majesty of God. He recognized, before anything else, God's
superiority and sovereignty. The greater God became to him,
the smaller his problems became. Our problem is, usually, that
when we're on top of the pile, we tend to lose a picture of God's
greatness, replacing it with our own.

Not Nehemiah.

The truly amazing part of this prayer is that Nehemiah
continued praying for four months. This guy prayed about the
situation for *16 weeks*. As he does so, he begins to get a clearer
picture of the issues. He also begins to understand the part he

is to play in the answer to his own prayer. All of that is evident from the way he closes verse 11 of chapter 1: *". . . Make Thy servant successful today, and grant him compassion before this man."*

As he prayed, it became obvious to him that he would have to take some action, so he began to formulate a long range plan. In verse 11 he asks God to allow that plan to succeed as he presents it to his boss, the king. His plan was to resign his position, leave Persia, and go to Jerusalem to rebuild the city.

Think about that. Nehemiah prayed for four months. *He waited* in other words. Do you? Are we inclined not only to pray, but also to wait? Those who do know that *waiting allows us to see with clearer perspective.*

But there is something else here. By becoming aware of what God wanted done through prayer, Nehemiah was led to *reorder his priorities*. He came to understand *his* role in solving the problems. He didn't come up with the role of others; it was his involvement that became clear to him. And that's why he was able to cut loose his ties, his career moorings, his time, and get involved. He was able to reorder his priorities and, at great personal loss, implement the changes. That is the story of the rest of the book.

When is the last time we did that? Not too many of us are into loss, are we? We are into other stuff. . .important stuff.

When have we reordered our priorities for spiritual reasons? Priorities like time in our life for God or time for our family. That company you slave for. . .if you were to drop dead tomorrow, they would replace you so fast it would make your head spin. Those committees you work on. . .same thing. But that is not true with your family. They will feel your loss so much longer and with much more pain.

Nehemiah prayed. . . .Nehemiah planned. . .and then he swung into action to meet the needs God had brought before him. In a very short time, he left Persia and headed west to Jerusalem to become personally involved in the despair and hopelessness of his people. Keep in mind, Nehemiah was 800 miles from Jerusalem in the days when the fastest means of travel was by horse or camel. . .across a desert. He could not choose among Amtrak, TWA, or Hertz. If his work party covered 15 miles per day, it would take a minimum of 53 traveling days just to get to Jerusalem. Think of the energy, the time, the cost. Think of the inconvenience involved for this man.

Yet, when your heart beats with love and concern, you never think of those things. And Nehemiah's heart was in Jerusalem.

For those of us who claim to be Christians, we have two very distinct courses available in life. One is to cultivate a small heart. It is the safest way to go because it minimizes the sorrows. If our ambition is to avoid the troubles of life, the formula is simple: minimize entangling relationships, carefully avoid elevated and noble ideals, and we will escape a host of afflictions.

The principle is true from any perspective. Cultivate deafness, and you will never hear the ugly things of life. Cultivate blindness, and you will never have to look at the ugly, unpleasant things of life. It is universally true for all of us that if we want to get through life with a minimum of trouble, we have only to reduce the compass of our hearts. This is how many people get through life. They have cultivated a smallness of heart, mind, and attitude.

But there is another path available to us. We can open ourselves up to others and become vulnerable. Enlarge your heart, cultivate a ministering heart, and you will enlarge your potential for pain. Little hearts are safe and protected, but they never contribute anything. No one ultimately benefits from restricted sympathies and limited vision. On the other hand, ministering hearts, though they are vulnerable, are also the hearts that know the most joy and leave their imprint on the world. Cultivate a small heart and there may be smoother sailing, but we will never see lives change and great things happen for God. [8]

Unfortunately, those who are willing to sacrifice personal time and convenience for others or for personal convictions are rare. Far too many Christians are filled with apathy and have eyes only for their own needs and struggles.

I know which group Nehemiah fell into. What about you? Cultivate a large heart. It always works.

Teddy Stallard would tell you that. Disinterested in school as he was, he wore musty, wrinkled clothes; his hair was never combed. He was one of those kids in school with a deadpan face, expressionless—sort of a glassy, unfocused stare. When Miss Thompson spoke to Teddy, he always answered in monosyllables. Unattractive, unmotivated, and distant, he was just plain hard to like. Even though his teacher said she loved each one in her fifth grade class the same, down inside, she knew she wasn't being completely truthful.

Whenever she marked Teddy's papers, she got a certain perverse pleasure out of putting Xs next to the wrong answers and when she put the Fs at the top of the papers, she always did it with a flair. She knew better; she had Teddy's records and she knew more about him than she wanted to admit. The record read:

> 1st Grade: Teddy shows promise with his work and attitude, but poor home situation.
>
> 2nd Grade: Teddy could do better. Mother is seriously ill. He receives little help at home.
>
> 3rd Grade: Teddy is a good boy but too serious. He is a slow learner. His mother died this year.

4th Grade: Teddy is very slow, but well-behaved.
His father shows no interest.

Christmas came and the boys and girls in Miss Thompson's class brought her Christmas presents. They piled their presents on her desk and crowded around to watch her open them. Among the presents there was one from Teddy Stallard. She was surprised that he had brought her a gift, but he had. Teddy's gift was wrapped in brown paper and was held together with Scotch tape. On the paper were written the simple words, "For Miss Thompson from Teddy." When she opened Teddy's present, out fell a gaudy rhinestone bracelet, with half the stones missing and a bottle of cheap perfume.

The other boys and girls began to giggle and smirk over Teddy's gifts, but Miss Thompson at least had enough sense to silence them by immediately putting on the bracelet and putting some of the perfume on her wrist. Holding her wrist up for the other children to smell, she said, "Doesn't it smell lovely?" And the children, taking their cue from the teacher, readily agreed with "oo's" and "ah's."

At the end of the day, when school was over and the other children had left, Teddy lingered behind. He slowly came over to her desk and said softly, "Miss Thompson. . .Miss Thompson, you smell just like my mother. . .and her bracelet looks real pretty on you, too. I'm glad you liked my presents." When Teddy left, Miss Thompson got down on her knees and asked God to forgive her.

The next day when the children came to school, they were welcomed by a new teacher. Miss Thompson had become a different person. She was no longer just a teacher; she had become an agent of God. She was now a person committed to loving her children and doing things for them that would live on after her. She helped all the children, but especially the slow ones, and especially Teddy Stallard. By the end of that school year, Teddy showed dramatic improvement. He had caught up with most of the students and was even ahead of some.

Miss Thompson didn't hear from Teddy for a long time. Then one day, she received a note that read:

Dear Miss Thompson:
I wanted you to be the first to know. I will be graduating second in my class.

Love,
Teddy Stallard

Four years later, another note came:

Dear Miss Thompson:
They just told me I will be graduating first in my class. I wanted you to be the first to know. The university has not been easy, but I liked it.

Love,
Teddy Stallard

And four years later:

Dear Miss Thompson:
As of today, I am Theodore Stallard, M.D. How about that? I wanted you to be the first to know. I am getting married next month, the 27th to be exact. I want you to come and sit where my mother would sit if she were alive. You are the only family I have; Dad died last year.

Love,
Teddy Stallard

Miss Thompson went to that wedding and sat where Teddy's mother would have sat. She deserved to sit there—even though she didn't feel like she did; but she had done something for Teddy that he could never forget. . . .[9]

She was his hero. . . .an ordinary person. . .an authentic, living example. . . .Are you. . .am I?

FOOTNOTES:

[1]Susanna McBee, *Heroes Are Back, U.S. News and World Report*, April 22, 1985, pp. 44-48.

[2]John W. Gardner, *The Antileadership Vaccine*, Annual Report of the Carnegie Corporation (New York, NY, Carnegie Corporation, 1965), p. 12.

[3]Charles C. Colton: Lacon, cited by Bergen Evans in the *Dictionary of Quotations* (Bonanza Books, New York, NY, 1968), p. 35:4.

[4]Cited by H. Edwin Young in *David: After God's Own Heart* (Broadman Press: Nashville, TN, 1984), pp. 36-37.

[5]*Moody Monthly* , Jan. 1987, p. 10.

[6]From *The Strong Willed Child* by James C. Dobson (Tyndale House Publishers, Inc., Wheaton, IL, 1978), pp. 137-138. Used by permission. All rights reserved.

[7]From the book *No Wonder They Call Him The Savior* by Max Lucado, copyright 1986 by Max Lucado. Published by Multnomah Press, Portland, OR 97266. Used by permission.

[8]R. Kent Hughes, *The Heart that Ministers (John 4:1-9)*, Published sermon, February 17, 1980, No. 12, The College Church in Wheaton, IL.

[9]Anthony Campolo, *Who Switched the Price Tags?* (Word Books, Dallas, TX, 1986), pp. 69-72. Used by permission.

CHAPTER TWO

PLAYING THE WAITING GAME
(Nehemiah 2:1-8)

The eminent theologian, Dr. Carl F. Henry said that, in his opinion, "The overriding issue of the 20th century is the crisis in authority."[1]

Another astute observer of our cultural playground is even stronger in his assessments. Listen:

Question authority! These words are not simply a bumper sticker slogan. They are fast becoming the unwritten motto of the 1980s. Let's face it; this generation is tough, not tender.

No longer is the voice of the parent respected in the home, is the sight of the policeman on the corner a model of courage and control, is the warning of the teacher in the classroom feared and obeyed, is the reprimand of the boss sufficient to bring about change, is the husband considered 'the head of the home.' (God help him if he even thinks such a thing!)

Ours is a talk-back, fight-back, get-even society that is ready to resist and sue at the slightest provocation. Defiance, resistance, violence and retaliation are now our "style." [2]

What makes this more emphatic a problem is the fact that all of us, to some degree, lead others. We are models and mentors to those around us. But, here is where the problem intensifies: Most of us also have to follow.

. . . Congregations are led and come under the authority of church leaders.

. . .Children and teenagers are led and come under the authority of their parents.

. . .Students are led by teachers, employees by employers.

. . .Wives by husbands, husbands by Christ.

And whether we enjoy it or not, that is the way life is. In fact, if you are in the 25-45 year-old bracket and working, or if you are older and now find yourself competing with that generation, experts tell us that the next several years will be characterized by scarce numbers of promotions, frustrated expectations and job hopping.

We saw the fruits of marriage hopping in the '80s. We've become a people of instant gratification who want complete freedom to follow the whim of the moment. Too many have never learned the discipline required to focus on a project and follow it through to completion. Millions of baby boomers who are now crowded on the first rungs of management will be forced to stay put, stuck on the ladder of advancement.

Now then, picture this scenario. You have a serious problem, and you have, what you consider to be, a potentially good plan or idea as to how to solve it. But, you need the approval of someone above you, someone in authority over you. How do you approach the problem?

Let's consider the role model that Nehemiah carves out for us in the second chapter of the Old Testament book that bears his name, because he walked through a very similar situation . . .and lived to talk about it.

When you find yourself itching to buck the system, eager to talk back, fight back, and do things the way you want to do them—regardless—then the first piece of counsel Nehemiah offers is that there are times *when we need to wait.*

Nehemiah knew that this was one of those times in his life. He needed, grafted into his bones, the quality of patience. Compare Nehemiah 1:1 and 2:1:

The words of Nehemiah the son of Hacaliah. Now it happened in the month Chislev, in the twentieth year, while I was in Susa the capitol. . . . And it came about in the month Nisan, in the twentieth year of King Artaxerxes, that wine was before him, and I took up the wine and gave it to the king. Now I had not been sad in his presence.

As these chapters open, the walls of the city of Jerusalem have been in ruins for 141 years. Nehemiah learned in chapter 1 that the wall of Jerusalem is broken down and its gates destroyed by fire. Since that news flash, Nehemiah has prayed about the problem. He also knows that as an employee of the king, the king is the key to the solution of his problem.

But keep in mind that there is a delay of four months from December (Chislev) when Nehemiah first heard the news, until April (Nisan) when he feels prepared to broach the subject to the king. Even though he was tightly connected to the king, he did not quickly or rashly blurt out a solution. He waited patiently.

Nehemiah was not a wimp. His personality was not passive, lethargic, or immobile. Dr. G. Campbell Morgan comments: *"The book [of Nehemiah] thrills and throbs and pulsates with the tremendous force of this man's will."* [3] But, still, he knew how to wait. With unhurried wisdom he bides his time for four months, constantly praying to God to grant the proper plan and the right opening. What amazes me about this is the fact that Nehemiah had great influence with the king. He has day-to-day access to him. Above all, by virtue of his position, he enjoyed the unreserved confidence of the king—but he still waits.

Have we learned how to wait? Or are we panic oriented? Trust is not impulsive, impatient, or easily frustrated. There are many times when we must wait before attempting to implement plans or ideas.

That's a difficult place to come to. In his book, *If God Cares,*

Why Do I Still Have Problems?, Dr. Ogilvie explains why.

> *The Latin root for the word "frustrate" means "to disappoint (or to be in vain).". . .Frustration is really a sense of powerlessness. It's a feeling of helplessness and hopelessness. We wonder if our best efforts will make any difference.*

And when that happens, we don't want to wait. We don't want to be patient. But when we are in a position where someone is in authority over us, we must learn to wait. Very often, however, people who have difficulty with authority, don't want to wait, not even on God. This exhibition of selfish immaturity focuses only on what they want.

Nehemiah had learned to adjust his own timetable to God's. But how did he learn that? Chapter 1, verse 1 gives us the answer: *"The words of Nehemiah the son of Hacaliah."* Now that doesn't mean much to us, but to the Hebrew it would, because Hacaliah's name means *"to wait for God."* Nehemiah's dad undoubtedly taught him to wait. Dads, what are we teaching our children? Would patience be on the list? Are we instilling into them the value of waiting for things? It's easy to imagine that Nehemiah's dad did that for him.

And it caught on, because it linked patience with a trust in God. Remember, the name Hacaliah means "to wait *for God.*"

Nehemiah undoubtedly knew the value of waiting because his dad had taught it to him and because he knew the character of God and could, therefore, have confidence in His sovereignty...His timing. We can see that clearly in Nehemiah's own words as he weaves throughout chapter 1 his *perspective* about God. Notice the first part of verse 5 and then verse 11 in chapter 1.

> *And I said, "I beseech Thee, O Lord God of heaven, the great and awesome God. . . . O Lord, I beseech Thee, may Thine ear be attentive to the prayer of Thy servant and the*

prayer of Thy servants who delight to revere Thy name, and make Thy servant successful today, and grant him compasssion before this man."

A.W. Tozer reminds us that: *"The essence of idolatry is the entertainment of thoughts about God that are unworthy of Him."* [4]

Nehemiah did not have those kinds of thoughts. Even as he prays, waiting for God to answer and to give him the right opportunity to speak to the king, Nehemiah's perspective is one of trust in the character and sovereignty of God. He goes out of his way to accentuate His confidence and reverence in the greatness of God. And that's the secret ingredient that turns us into ordinary heroes who stand in their places for God. The more I learn about God, the greater confidence I have for trusting Him. That's what Nehemiah says in verse 5. The Hebrew word *"great"* comes from a verb that means *"to twist a rope, to make firm or strong."* As Nehemiah reflected on the greatness of God, as he worshipped Him, his trust in God made him stronger and able to wait. He knew that God had his best interests at heart, that He loved him, and was working out His will in Nehemiah's life.

Nehemiah could wait patiently because of his trust in God and God's timing. And if we have that kind of trust in that kind of God, then it must impact our day-to-day *performance*. It certainly did for Nehemiah. Read again verse 1 of chapter 2:

And it came about in the month Nisan, in the twentieth year of King Artaxerxes, that wine was before him, and I took up the wine and gave it to the king. Now I had not been sad in his presence.

In the Persian court of that day, you were expected to present a positive image. Regardless of what kinds of problems you were wrestling with, you were not expected to wear your emotions on your sleeve. And Nehemiah has done just that.

The text says that he has not been *"sad"* in the presence of the king before. The word means *"unhappy or depressed visibly."* In some places in the Old Testament, the word can also mean *"displeasing or evil."* In other words, despite his intense identification with the problem in Jerusalem, Nehemiah did not allow it to affect his on-the-job performance. He didn't do anything displeasing to the king. He didn't call in sick; he didn't complain; he didn't moan about how bad his job is; he didn't cut back on his efforts.

When we really trust in the character of God and His sovereignty, it impacts our day-to-day performance, whether at work, at home, in front of our family, or with friends. Regardless of the situation, there ought to be a quality of attitude difference for the Christian.

U.S. News & World Report (Dec. 9, 1985) cited an estimate that in any one year American workers steal $160 billion from their employers by arriving late, leaving early, and misusing time on the job. And Christians are included in those statistics, too. Instead of trust, we moan, sulk, whine, enter a protracted state of depression, or we flip those around and become irritable, hostile, pushy, and ulcerated.

Maxine Hancock, in her book *The Forever Principle*, said it well: *"The Christian sense of vocation lies in knowing that over and above circumstances, union bosses, employers, and drive gears of machinery or bureaucracy, we can serve the Lord Jesus Christ. . . ."*

If we checked with your employer today, how would he evaluate your presence and contribution? If we could talk to your co-workers, friends, your children, your foreman, your fellow church members—what words would they choose to describe you? Can you wait? Are you patient with plans? Does your perspective of trust in God shine through? And does it impact your day-to-day performance?

Nehemiah had that perspective of trust. He knew that God was with him and was able to wait. But that didn't mean he would never put his plan before the king. In Nehemiah 1:11, he prays for the best opportunity to present the idea to the king so that it would be well received. That time comes in verse 2 of chapter 2.

So the king said to me, "Why is your face sad though you are not sick? This is nothing but sadness of heart." Then I was very much afraid.

Having maintained a positive demeanor and performance for all the years of his service, Nehemiah sensed that this day was the correct time to present his request to the king. It took genuine courage to approach one of the Persian rulers and to allow his true feelings to be obvious. But Nehemiah did, and the king respected Nehemiah's past performance enough to ask immediately about it.

But even before he gives his answer, Nehemiah demonstrates his tremendous respect for his boss. Look at verses 2 and 3. "Then I was very much afraid. . . . " Nehemiah was frightened for a number of reasons. First of all, he knew that the king had already stopped the rebuilding of the walls of Jerusalem. What would he think of this new request? Nehemiah was sensitive to the fact that bringing up new business wasn't always a good idea. That shows respect for the king's position and opinion. He was afraid, also, because he simply recognized the king as the final authority. He understood the lines of authority and accountability. But he was afraid, too, because even though he sensed that this was the correct moment to bring the subject up, he knew that betraying his emotions before the king could bring severe punishment. Nehemiah does not for a second come flippantly or casually to the king. He comes with respect.

Consider verse 3: "I said to the king, 'Let the king live

forever.' " The expression, *"let the king live forever,"* was a common form of respectful address, assuring the king of loyalty and respect. And even as the king asks what it is that Nehemiah wants, notice the way that Nehemiah prefaces his request in the first part of verse 5: *And I said to the king, "If it please the king and if your servant has found favor before you, send me to Judah, to the city of my father's tombs, that I may rebuild it."*

First, Nehemiah breathed a silent prayer to God—undoubtedly for the right words—took a deep breath. . .and began. The word *"please"* here means *"agreeable or joyful."* In other words, as good as he thinks his idea is, he wants the king to agree with it, not just say it's OK. He wants him to like the idea, and, notice, he says, *"If it pleases the king,"* not, *"Since this pleases me."* By beginning his request this way, Nehemiah preserves the king's superiority. The king does not feel threatened or pressured. Nehemiah was inviting him to make a decision.

How about you? How do you speak to those in authority over you? When you come to your boss, do you show that kind of respect and loyalty? Or do you simply come and inform him of the way you want it done? Do you come to him after you've already taken the action and it's too late to reverse things, but you wanted him to be informed? Some of us don't even want to ask. We just do our thing with no respect. Too often, we approach God the same way, arguing by our attitude with His wisdom and sovereignty. Do we respect God's authority?

Nehemiah understood respect for authority, both human and divine. And that helped him as he presented his request. But so did some other things.

Nehemiah outlined the problem for the king in verse 3: *"Why should my face not be sad when the city, the place of my fathers' tombs, lies desolate, and its gates have been consumed by fire?"*

Now notice what happens in verse 4: *"The king said to me,*

35

'What would you request?' So I prayed to the God of heaven."

Nehemiah prayed before he spoke. That is a great model. All of us have been in similar spots. We've anticipated talking to someone, of laying our plans out on the table, and then the moment hits and we gulp, the palms start to sweat, we feel a little queazy. What should we do? Pray. One commentator observed:

> *This is a terrific example of spontaneous prayer. Before turning to answer the king, Nehemiah utters a brief prayer to God. Despite his fear, he knew that first and foremost he was not simply standing in the presence of an earthly king, but before the King of heaven.* [5]

This is important for every Christian. We, too, need to ask the Lord for special help or direction before going into a committee meeting, before presenting a controversial proposition to our employer, before handling a trying customer, before entering delicate negotiations with a manufacturer or supplier, before addressing a problem with a teacher, or discussing a difficulty with our spouse.

And keep in mind, Nehemiah, as he prayed this time, probably did not close his eyes. He certainly did not hit his knees or go into a closet or look for a church. And you can bet he didn't pray very long. When a king asks for an answer, falling on your knees with your eyes closed for a long time is not a real bright thing to do. More than likely, Nehemiah, standing in an attitude of prayer shot an arrow to heaven that may have simply said, *"Lord God, help me to say the right things."*

And he did. Notice verse 5 this time:

> *And I said to the king, "If it please the king, and if your servant has found favor before you, send me to Judah, to the city of my fathers' tombs, that I may rebuild it."*

Nehemiah bases his request on his past performance. We've

already caught a glimpse of this in verse 1. But the point is, Nehemiah was confident in the quality of his work, not just in the past four months, but long before that. He had set a standard of excellence at work. He knew his personnel file would reveal that he worked hard, met his deadlines, completed assignments, and that he followed directives. Does ours?

Current research indicates that fewer than one out of every four job holders say that they are currently working at full potential. One-half admit that they do not put effort into their job over and above what is required to hold onto it. The overwhelming majority, 75 percent, indicate that they could be significantly more effective than they are presently; and close to six out of every ten Americans on the job believe that they *"do not work as hard as they used to."* [6] Being a Christian doesn't seem to make much difference.

Not so with Nehemiah. His request was preceded by prayer and a life of integrity and godly character. It was based on his track record in the past, and it was incredibly well prepared. Notice verse 6:

> *Then the king said to me, the queen sitting beside him, "How long will your journey be, and when will you return?" So it pleased the king to send me, and I gave him a definite time.*

Nehemiah has carefully thought through what he would need to do the job, to solve the problem. When asked about his needs, he begins by telling the king how long it would take to get things in order—he was gone 12 years, by the way. According to verse 7, he thought far enough ahead to ask the king for safe-conduct letters (our equivalent of a passport). Verse 8 tells us that he was also very much aware of the physical items he needed to do the job. He's checked out the territory around Jerusalem, and he located a Home Depot, or as the text translates it, one of the king's forests—just six miles south of the city where the best lumber for building was found. He even knew the name of the man in charge. He hadn't wasted any of the hours in the four months he'd waited.

When you have a plan, when you have an idea that needs cooperation at home, at school, at work, at church, don't wing it; don't try to fake it. Be prepared. Present a problem with a proposed solution.

Notice one final thing. It's at the end of verse 8. We've seen Nehemiah's approach to a problem. It involved incredible planning and exquisite timing. He has done all of that and more. We're not surprised that the king gave him what he asked. Now, notice the end of verse 8.

And the king granted this to me because I was so well-prepared, because my annual reviews were of such quality, and because I was such a diplomat.

That's not what it says, is it? No. Notice who gets the credit...God, not Nehemiah. *"And the king granted them to me because the good hand of my God was on me."*

There is no limit to what God can accomplish through the person who does not care who gets the credit, who does not jump for the spotlight, even when warranted, who does not look for ways to flaunt those in authority, to resist, to fight. Rather, God works through those who maintain a quiet humility in the presence of the God they trust and reverence. That was Nehemiah. He models so well these words from the prophet Jeremiah:

Thus says the Lord, "Let not a wise man boast of his wisdom, and let not the mighty man boast of his might, let not a rich man boast of his riches; but let him who boasts boast of this, that he understands and knows Me, that I am the Lord who exercises lovingkindness, justice, and righteousness on earth; for I delight in these things," declares the Lord. (Jeremiah 9:23-24)

FOOTNOTES:

[1]Cited by J. Robertson McQuilkin, "The Power Struggle," Bulletin of Wheaton College, in *The Christian Reader,* January/February 1979, p. 2.

[2]Charles R. Swindoll, *Strengthening Your Grip,* (Word, Inc., Dallas, TX, 1982), pp. 237-238. Used with permission.

[3]*The Living Messiah of the Books of the Bible–Old Testament*, G.C. Morgan, (Fleming H. Revell Co., Old Tappan, NJ, 1912), p. 262 and cited in *Nehemiah: Expositors Bible Commentary*, Vol. 4, (Zondervan Corporation, Grand Rapids, MI, 1988).

[4]A.W. Tozer, *The Knowledge of the Holy,* (Harper and Row, New York, NY, 1961), p. 11.

[5]Edwin Yamauchi, *Nehemiah: Expositers Bible Commentary,* Vol. 4, (Zondervan Corporation, Grand Rapids, MI, 1988), p. 685.

[6]Warren Bennis and Burt Nanus, *Leaders—The Strategies For Taking Charge*, (Harper and Row; New York, NY, 1985), pp. 7-8.

CHAPTER THREE

WHEN THINGS LOOK GRIM
(Nehemiah 2:10-21)

Not one person reading this has had a problem-free week. If we are fortunate, we can sometimes manage two or three days without a crisis, without a persistent problem. But then, just as the smoke begins to clear, another fire begins to burn. And our problems are not predictable. They come in all sizes and varieties. Leo Buscaglia, in his book, *Bus 9 to Paradise*, describes one of those recurring problems. This is how he views it:

I must confess that there are certain occurrences in my house that defy any rational explanation. For instance, one of the great and perpetual mysteries is where my socks disappear. I can't seem to keep a matching pair. I am continually having to buy new socks. After the first wash, some of them simply vanish.

They never go in pairs, which wouldn't be so bad. The annoying thing is that I am left with one green sock, one blue and one black. I have accumulated a huge pile which I dare not throw out lest a matching sock reappear as mysteriously as it disappeared. So far, this hasn't happened.

They certainly can't just walk off. Or can they?. . .I've checked the machines for teeth, for escape hatches or mysterious tubes that might eat up or siphon off my socks. This would account for the mystery, but there are no such things in either the washer or dryer. . .I still suspect (however) a phantom somewhere in the laundry room just waiting for the rinse cycle to end.

I have found that the sock problem has reached epidemic proportions all over the United States. I am not alone. Friends and family, men and women alike, from all over the country, have offered comfort and helpful suggestions. There were the practical people who have suggested that I simply pin, staple or use string to keep socks together. I've even been told of commercially made clips which guaranteed that the socks would come out as they went in, two by two.

An artist suggested that being fearful of mixing colors is a cultural hang-up. She encouraged me to wear mismatched socks fearlessly. "The more outrageous the color combinations the better," she said, "like flowers in a garden." A less daring person solved the problem by purchasing all his socks in the same color. . . .A scientist assures me that it has been scientifically proven that socks disappear and coat hangers keep proliferating because socks are the larvae of coat hangers.

In 1975, even the cartoonist Jules Feiffer, expressed his puzzlement about missing socks. In his cartoon, his pathetic figure gets down to his last two pair of socks, when his washing machine sends him a message which reads, "Quit trifling with the laws of nature and bring me more socks." [1]

All of us understand day-to-day problems and frustrations. Sometimes these problems and frustrations are connected to circumstances or things, like washing machines and lost socks and although they may upset us emotionally, in many cases they are manageable. But they move from the frustrating, yet manageable level, to the gut-wrenching and seemingly impossible level when we add to them the most frequently recurring problem of life: dealing with difficult people. When you put together a problem of circumstance and a problem with people, that is when things start to look grim, as they did for Nehemiah in chapter 2 of his story.

We already are aware of his problem of circumstance. The walls of the city of Jerusalem are in ruins, and it is his vision to see the city rebuilt. But that is just the beginning of the problems. In verse 9 of chapter 2, we see a *prelude to further difficulties* for Nehemiah. Pick up the story with me there:

> *Then I came to the governors of the provinces beyond the River and gave them the king's letters. Now the king had sent with me officers of the army and horsemen.*

Remember, Nehemiah had asked the king for passports so that he could travel through various countries. He had asked for letters of introduction to key people in Jerusalem so that supplies could be ordered and the work begun quickly. And, of course, he had respectfully asked for the permission to leave his job for this new venture. And that is what he received. But additionally, the king gave Nehemiah an armed escort. To ensure Nehemiah's authority and safety, the king made a decision to send along a military convoy. Nehemiah had not asked for that, but the king provided them. That's a pretty clear message that the king sensed that there was going to be trouble ahead. And there was. We catch our first glimpse of it in verse 10, and, significantly, it is a people-related problem. Notice our introduction to it:

> *And when Sanballat the Horonite and Tobiah the Ammonite official heard about it, it was very displeasing to them that someone had come to seek the welfare of the sons of Israel.*

These two men, Sanballat and Tobiah, throw a long and dark shadow over the rest of the book. Both of them were men of influence and power. Sanballat, whose name means "sin has given life," was the governor of Samaria, the province just north of Jerusalem. He immediately becomes Nehemiah's chief opponent. Tobiah governed the country to the east, called Ammon, but as a Jew, he had tight family connections in Jerusalem. In fact, some of his own relatives ultimately formed part of the construction crew in the rebuilding project. The astounding thing about these two men is their religious identification.

One of the premier Old Testament scholars of our day, Dr. R.K. Harrison, says that: *"Sanballat, along with Tobiah (were) probably regarded by some of (their) contemporaries as being at least as devout a Jew as Ezra or Nehemiah."* [2]

They were supposed to be spiritual giants.

But as Nehemiah rolled into town, they saw their territory being invaded. This was their turf, and they did not want any outside interference, especially if it meant that their personal influence and power might be diminished.

One of the most common and frustrating problems with people is dealing with those who feel threatened by you. If you are new in an office setting, you may have spotted some Sanballats and Tobiahs in their reactions to you. The same thing occurs in church. Sometimes there are those who are threatened by newcomers. They are afraid you will diminish their influence and popularity, so they give you an un-welcome mat.

But there is more to this than just that. Sometimes, people who view themselves as influential, spiritual, and powerful become upset with us because we don't acknowledge that influence, that spirituality, that power, and we don't fall down in awe of who they are. That may have been part of the problem here. But I think there is even more than that. Look again at the end of verse 10. *"They were very much disturbed that someone had come to promote the welfare of the Israelites."*

The term "welfare" means "the benefit or the happiness" of someone. That is what Nehemiah was here for—the benefit and the happiness and the safety of the Jewish people.

Isn't it interesting that people can be upset with you for caring about the welfare of others? You reach out to someone in friendship, or counsel, or simply give attention and help, and somebody else sees that, or hears about it, and amazingly, they become upset with you. Why? Because they feel deprived. What you are doing for someone else is what they want from you. And so they are jealous. Instead of being thrilled that you care enough to help someone, they interpret your actions as not caring about them. Nehemiah's problem with the rebuilding of the walls of Jerusalem was intensified because of his concern for people, a concern that had made him risk his life, his position, and travel 800 miles to do something he saw as important for God and God's people. The jealousy and resistance of Sanballat and Tobiah is the kind that makes you want to run away and hide and forget about your concern for others. How unfortunate, and yet how common.

So, who are you upset with? Have you reacted like Sanballat or Tobiah to newcomers on your turf? Or does a love for people—strangers and friends—make you welcome them?

Although trouble was brewing for Nehemiah, he had a city to rebuild, and he had negative people to confront. So he kept on with the task. But he used a *perceptive approach* in dealing with his problems. And the first element of that approach is that he began with *caution.*

So I came to Jerusalem and was there three days. And I arose in the night, I and a few men with me. I did not tell any one what my God was putting into my mind to do for Jerusalem and there was no animal with me except the animal on which I was riding. . . . And the officials did not know where I had gone or what I had done; nor had I as yet told the Jews, the priests, the nobles, the officials, or the rest who did the work (9:11-12,16).

Nehemiah took time to get his bearing—three days, in fact. He did not plunge immediately into problem solving. During those three days he probably rested so that he would be fresh and on top of things when he needed to get rolling. Probably he used this time to refine his plan for rebuilding the wall and to formulate the best approach for dealing with Sanballat and Tobiah.

But observe from verse 12 that Nehemiah isn't panicked about Sanballat and Tobiah nor the immensity of his task. He doesn't immediately run out and talk about his problems or his plans. Instead, he proceeds carefully and discreetly. That makes even more sense if you're tired. Nehemiah, when confronted with problems of circumstances and people, knew enough to get some rest. After the three days have passed, he sets his alarm for midnight, and while everyone else is sawing logs, he and a very few trusted associates begin to inspect the city. But he doesn't tell anyone what he is up to. He doesn't advertise his plans or invite attack by doing his inspection in broad daylight, and he does not invite leaks by prematurely letting others in on his plan. Nehemiah is acutely aware of waiting for the right moment to tell the people his plans, and he wisely keeps them to himself until he is ready to act.

One of the reasons why he did this was his conviction that the project was not his. It was from God, and it was for the benefit of God's people. It was not from Nehemiah nor for his prestige. J. Oswald Sanders writes in his book, *Spiritual Leadership:*

The leader must be one, who, while welcoming the friendship and support of all who can offer it, has sufficient inner resources to stand alone even in the face of fierce opposition. In the discharge of his responsibilities, he or she must be prepared to have no one but God. [3]

So it was with Nehemiah. But don't miss the principle that Nehemiah modeled when facing a problem: Whatever you do, don't talk about a problem prematurely. When we face problems, the first mistake we usually make is to talk about them with too many people, too soon. We need to keep a lid on things. We intensify our problems when we prematurely involve other people.

Look at the kinds of people he kept in the dark: *"And the officials did not know where I had gone or what I had done; nor had I as yet told the Jews, the priests, the nobles, the officials or the rest who did the work"* (verse 16).

The nobles were heavy hitters in the city, the guys who directed public affairs. The officials were those who ran the city government, at whatever level it was maintained. The priests covered the spiritual areas of religion and worship. The Jews were his countrymen. Nehemiah didn't tell anyone. When we open our mouths too soon, we can get in trouble. Usually, we haven't had time to think carefully or pray regularly, and what we share usually ends up being inaccurate, because, given some time and additional thought we may change our minds and/or alter our course of action.

Nehemiah's approach to his problems began with caution, which he then followed with *an accurate assessment* of the situation. That's verses 13 through 18:

So I went out at night by the Valley Gate in the direction of the Dragon's Well and on to the Rufuse Gate, inspecting the walls of Jerusalem which were broken down and its gates which were consumed by fire. Then I passed on to the Fountain Gate and the King's Pool, but there was no place for my mount to pass. So I went up at night by the ravine and inspected the wall. Then I entered the Valley Gate again and returned. . . .Then I said to them, "You see the bad situation we are in, that Jerusalem is desolate and its gates burned by fire. Come, let us rebuild the wall of Jerusalem that we may no longer be a reproach." And I told them how the hand of my God had been favorable to me, and also about the king's words which he had spoken to me. Then they said, "Let us arise and build." So they put their hands to the good work.

In order to deal with problems in our lives, we must have all the facts. We must study the situation meticulously, not jump to conclusions. That is why Nehemiah personally conducts his own inspection tour of the perimeter of the city walls. He wanted first-hand information about the problem. And he wanted it to be accurate information. His inspection was designed to do just that. In fact, the Hebrew text of verse 13 literally reads, *"I examined INTO the walls,"* meaning that Nehemiah examined the damage closely. The verb comes from a medical term used by a surgeon to describe his intense and precise examination as he probes a wound.

That's the nature of Nehemiah's assessment of the problem. And it is only when he is in possession of all the facts that he convenes a meeting of the people in verse 17. *Then I said to them, "You see the bad situation we are in, that Jerusalem is desolate and its gates burned by fire. Come, let us rebuild the wall of Jerusalem that we may no longer be a reproach."*

The principle that emerges visibly from these verses is: In order to deal with problems, we must have all the facts. We must have personal access to all the information that is available, not suppositions, not hearsay, not gossip or exaggeration—facts.

Then if those facts substantiate the fact that there really is a problem, then the second part of the principle surfaces. In order to solve problems, we must admit that we have problems. That is what Nehemiah helps the people to see in verse 17. It was necessary for these people to be reawakened to see their real need, so Nehemiah begins by focusing on the problem.

Sometimes when we are inundated by problems and we don't seem to be able to find a solution, we tend to give up trying. We subconsciously pretend there is no problem. That's where many of these people were. So the first thing Nehemiah does as he talks to them is to remind them there is a problem. Because unless their problem situation was freely admitted, no remedy could be adopted.

But notice also, that Nehemiah identified himself with the problem. *"You see the bad situation we are in."* The most natural reaction for Nehemiah, after he has surveyed the damage, would be to get everyone together and say, *"Man, this place is a disaster....*You *have a major problem."* After all, he had been 800 miles away.

We all tend to do that. We want to ease out of problems. We want to blame our marriage difficulties on our spouse, our teenagers' educational deficiencies on their teachers, our addiction to medication on our physicians, our financial woes on the lack of proper pay, our church construction inconvenience on our board or senior pastor. Not Nehemiah. The problem was his also. And by identifying himself with the people in that way, they were more responsive to his recommendation for *action.*

There was no more time for weeping and whining about the problems of the moment; it was time to act. And Nehemiah, based on his examination of the situation, lays out the plan he has formulated crisply and clearly. . .*"Let's build the thing!"* He doesn't complicate the process by offering 15 possible solutions. He has one plan. . .Plan A. He doesn't confuse the issue by using terminology no one could grasp. He is simple and to the point.

Nor does he say, *"Well, we're in a tough spot here, and I'm really not too sure what to do. Maybe we could try this; do you think?"* That's not Nehemiah. He knows how to take a definite course of action.

When you face a problem, form a plan, then act. Don't waffle around. Ted Engstrom, in one of his books, writes:

*Once a decision is made, don't look back or second
guess yourself. Expect and demand commitment to the
decision on your part and on the part of those who are
going to be working on it. . . .Be consistent in applying the
consequences of your decision, but don't vacillate. [4]*

Nehemiah didn't. Faced with problems of circumstance and
people, he approached them calmly and with caution. He
gathered all the facts before he mentioned the problems or
announced a plan of action. Now, does that mean all his
problems are over? Not on your life. The rest of the book is a
record of more problems. But, underlying all of those are three
persistent realities that Nehemiah understood and models for
us in verses 18-20 of chapter 2.

The first reality is what we might term *a proper motivation*
to face our problems.

*And I told them how the hand of my God had been
favorable to me, and also about the king's words which he
had spoken to me. Then they said, "Let us arise and build."
So they put their hands to the good work* (verse 18).

To his plan of action, Nehemiah now adds encouragement.
He explains all that happened while he was in Persia working
for the king and how God had not only opened the way for him
to come to Jerusalem, but had also provided the materials for
the repairing of the wall. Nehemiah reminded the people that
God was alive and active on their behalf. By pointing them
away from their fears, Nehemiah focuses their minds on what
God is doing for them; and they realize, for the first time in a
long time, that God is on their side. That's when they became
involved. And notice, as they did, the problem of a ruined city
now became *"this good work."* When our motivation is godly,
our perspective becomes positive.

To face the continuing onslaught of problems in our lives we
must ***know our God is with us in the midst of these problems***

and remember His faithfulness to us in the past. To borrow again from the well-worn pen of J. Oswald Sanders: *"Nehemiah raised the morale of his colleagues. He achieved this end by stimulating their faith and directing their thoughts away from the magnitude of their immediate problems to the greatness and trustworthiness of God."* [5]

And the response of the people, as we've noted, was electric. At the end of verse 18 they replied, *"Let us arise and build."*

The walls of Jerusalem had been in ruins for over 140 years. The leaders and people had become resigned to their situation, and it took someone like Nehemiah to come in, assess the situation, and rally the people to do something about the problem. And he did it by reminding them of the greatness of their God. . .not Nehemiah. I wonder how many of our problems, which we are resigned to, which we see as hopeless and without solution, would turn around if our focus on our God intensified? That's the first persistent reality.

There is a second reality. . .*persistent criticism.*

But when Sanballat the Horonite, and Tobiah the Ammonite official, and Geshem the Arab heard it, they mocked us and despised us and said, "What is this thing you are doing? Are you rebelling against the king?" (verse 19)

You knew that Sanballat and Tobiah would resurface sooner or later. Now they're doing what they are best at, throwing verbal darts. The verb *"mocked"* suggests that they kept repeating the same lines, day after day. Every time they did it, they looked down their noses at Nehemiah and his friends. That's the emphasis of the word *"despised."* They really thought they were something. Critics usually do.

Had you lived in Nehemiah's era, where would you find yourself? With Nehemiah or against him? Getting on with the work or criticizing it?

But notice something else here. This second round of personality-related problems is more intense than the first ones back in verse 10. Here in verse 19, Sanballat and Tobiah have added a partner in crime, a guy named Geshem. Who's he? Well, he and his son are in charge of a powerful group of people, who, under the Persian government, controlled land as far away as Egypt. Additionally, they operated a lucrative import/export business in the area. So Geshem has political influence and money. Notice that together they lie about Nehemiah, accusing him of rebelling against the king, even though Nehemiah carried with him letters of permission from the king.

When you are a critic and your influence is waning and your tactics aren't working, lobbying always helps. And when you know that the truth is against you, lies and deceit are the only tools you have left. At that point, most critics will say anything to win their point. As difficult as it may be to accept, that is the second persistent reality. Once a person or a group begins to do something for God's glory, criticism and opposition are only a stone's throw away. All godly actions meet with strong resistance.

And that is why the third persistent reality is so important. It is the need for *ongoing courage* in the face of problems. Nehemiah had it.

So I answered them and said to them, "The God of heaven will give us success; therefore we His servants will arise and build, but you have no portion, right, or memorial in Jerusalem " (verse 20).

Nehemiah's answer was brief, but very firm. He serves notice on his enemies that he will not be intimidated. He courageously confronts those who are attempting to stop what God is doing.

Dr. Warren Wiersbe says:

[That's] the kind of leader we really need. He has the courage to face the problems honestly, the wisdom to

understand them, the strength to do something about them, and the faith to trust God to do the rest. He isn't afraid of losing friends or making enemies. He can't be intimidated by threats or bought with bribes. He is God's man, and he isn't for sale. [6]

FOOTNOTES:

[1]Leo Buscaglia, *Bus 9 to Paradise*, (William Morrow and Company, Inc., New York, NY, 1986), pp. 117, 119-120. Used by permission.

[2]R.K. Harrison, *Introduction to the Old Testament*, (William B. Eerdmans, Grand Rapids, MI, 1969), p. 1141.

[3]J. Oswald Sanders, *Spiritual Leadership*, (Moody Press, Chicago, IL, 1967), p. 108.

[4]Ted Engstrom and Edward R. Dayton, *The Art of Management for Christian Leaders*, (Word Books, Dallas, TX, 1979), p. 154.

[5]J. Oswald Sanders, Ibid., p. 155.

[6]Warren W. Wiersbe, *The Integrity Crisis*, (Oliver-Nelson Books, Nashville, TN, 1988), pp. 73-74.

CHAPTER FOUR

WHEN CRITICISM STARTS...
(Nehemiah 4:1-9)

You don't have to have lived very long before you are awakened to the fact that you can never escape disapproval, regardless of how much you may want it to go away. For every opinion you have, someone somewhere has exactly the opposite view.

Abraham Lincoln once talked about this in a conversation at the White House: *"If I were to read, much less to answer all the attacks made on me, this shop might as well be closed for any other business. I do the very best I know how—the very best I can, and I mean to keep doing so until the end. If the end brings me out all right, what is said against me won't amount to anything. If the end brings me out wrong, ten angels swearing I was right would make no difference."* [1]

Criticism, real or imagined can run and ruin your life. It almost did that to Nehemiah. In the fourth chapter of Nehemiah—the guns of the critics are aimed full force at him and his friends. It's a scene that leaves me weak, but it's a lesson in reality that all of us must face...when the hurricane of criticism is hurled our way.

And it will be. But part of our ability to deal with criticism, at least to some extent, is *knowing how to spot the critic.* Because there are certain operating procedures that critics use, there are certain characteristics of criticism to which we must be alert.

The first is that *criticism inevitably accompanies positive activities.* Notice the last part of Nehemiah 2:18—the people's response to Nehemiah's challenge to rebuild the walls of the city of Jerusalem: "Let us arise and rebuild."

They're ready to go with the project, and chapter 3 lists everyone who participated. So in chapter 3, verse 1 we see,

Then Eliashib the high priest arose with his brothers the priests and built the Sheep Gate; they consecrated it and hung its doors. They consecrated the wall to the Tower of the Hundred and the Tower of Hananel.

The word *consecrated* means *"to set apart as sacred."* The priests, as soon as they completed their work, dedicated the repaired gate, wall, and towers to God. The priests, from the outset, wanted to declare their solemn belief that the very stones and timbers of Jerusalem belonged to God. What a great attitude! And everyone listed in chapter 3 agreed—with one exception: *"Moreover, next to him the Tekoites made repairs, but their nobles did not support the work of their masters"* (3:5).

In the Hebrew language it literally reads, *"they did not bring their neck to service."* Meaning, they refused to subject themselves to the service of anyone else. But what is more, the expression, as used here, indicates a hidden resentment against the leadership of Nehemiah. And because it was his idea, they wouldn't go along with it. . .even if it was a good one. A task that should have been seen as sacred, as positive. . .as God ordained. . .was not.

That's because criticism often surfaces when positive things are happening. Robert Foster put it this way in his book, *The Navigator:*

The mists of criticism do hang about a mountain. Men who want no mists must be content with plains and deserts. Mists come with mountains. Soon the mists will evaporate, and the mountain will stand out in all its grandeur in the morning sunlight. Multitudes will stay in the valley, for there are few who will aspire to reach the summit. [2]

Nehemiah did. . .and the mists of criticism rolled in. These people did not want to serve. And if you do not have a servant's heart—you tend not to cooperate. . .you tend to criticize. Is that true of you? Like these people. . .do you stand in opposition to good suggestions, good ideas, simply because you resent the person who made the suggestion? Do you tend to criticize something that ought to bring thankfulness to God from your heart? Or does it go even deeper than that. . .you just basically don't want to help anyone but yourself? You may want the benefits of the idea, but you won't support it. That's the first identifying mark of the critic.

There is another mark of a critic and that is that *criticism is often hostile* and *vocal*. Dr. Donald Campbell, president of Dallas Seminary, puts it this way:

> *How do we account for such vicious and unrelenting attacks as are recorded in the next three chapters of this book, attacks that originated both externally and internally? Simply, that Satan tries to oppose the work of God in any way he can.* [3]

Chapter 4 verse 1: *"When Sanballat heard that we were rebuilding the wall, he became furious and very angry and mocked the Jews. . . . "*

The Hebrew word describes a physical burning sensation in the throat as the result of anger. Sanballat was absolutely beside himself with rage when he observed the progress on the wall because he knew that the success of the project would undermine his authority and influence. We can almost watch his blood pressure come to a boil as bitter and determined resentment builds inside of him. David Augsburger offers this insight into bitterness and resentment:

> *What a strange thing bitterness is!. . .It slowly sets, like a permanent plaster cast, perhaps protecting the wearer from further pain but ultimately holding him rigid in*

frozen animation. His feelings and responses have turned to concrete, and, like concrete, they're all mixed up and firmly set.

Bitterness is paralysis. [4]

That describes Sanballat and some of us. And when it does, we are out of control. Our anger controls us and we lose all sense of perception and judgment. When that happens, when uncontrolled anger invades and dominates, you can be assured of one thing: *that anger will be expressed.* It will take some form of negative action. Usually through our words. Anger frequently translates itself into verbal criticism of others. It did with Sanballat. According to verse 1 he begins to ridicule Nehemiah and his friends. A little later in the account, Sanballat's anger has spread like a cancer to others, and together they plot their actions (4:7-8).

Now it came about when Sanballat, Tobiah, the Arabs, the Ammonites, and the Ashdodites heard that the repair of the walls of Jerusalem went on, and that the breaches began to be closed, they were very angry. And all of them conspired together to come and fight against Jerusalem and to cause a disturbance in it.

That's what you do to people when you're angry and not in control. The moment that Sanballat knew that Nehemiah and the people were building, he was livid. And he vented his rage through his speech.

John Edward Lantz, in his book *Speaking in the Church,* warns us about this: *"Every person, even one's closest friend, has the potential of becoming ferocious, and of fighting his opponent to the bitter end. He may do so with. . .deceit, intrigue, lies, gossip, open attack, or in any other way which seems expedient to him at the time. Expediency is the first law of life for most of the people, most of the time."* [5]

Does that describe you? For whatever reasons, you're a

bitter, resentful, and angry person. Don't kid yourself. You cannot hide your anger forever. Sooner or later it will boil over inside of you and, like a scalding cauldron, it will produce a flow of verbal criticism toward others.

Criticism often accompanies positive times. Criticism is usually hostile and vocal. But in addition, you can spot a critic pretty easily because *critics do not operate alone. . .critics run with other critics.*

In Nehemiah 4:2, when Sanballat starts to shoot his mouth off, his audience consists of his fellow officials, including his favorite yes-man, Tobiah, and the soldiers from Samaria—the troops he would have under his direction as governor. In other words, he is speaking publicly before his associates and subordinates. But then the circle of critics expands.

In chapter 2, the attacks came initially from Sanballat and Tobiah, the Ammonite official. Then, by the end of that chapter, Geshem the Arab had joined the party. But now in Nehemiah 4:7, there is not only Sanballat and Tobiah the Ammonite. . .but also other Ammonites, encouraged no doubt by Tobiah. You'll also notice that it is not simply Geshem the Arab. Now it includes other Arabs, incited by Geshem. And then we are introduced to the Ashdodites, a new group. They come from a city over 60 miles away on the Mediterranean coast. As descendants of the Philistines—the historical enemies of Israel—it is likely that Sanballat aroused that old hatred and drew them into the attack.

Critics never operate as independents. Critics need an audience; they need others to listen to their complaints. And it really doesn't matter to them who listens, just as long as somebody listens and they gather a following. Critics, by their very nature, are proud and angry people. They do not keep criticism to themselves. They must draw others into the fray. In doing so they feel important again. They feel like they are the center of things. . .

that the spotlight is finally back where it belongs. . .on them.

But critics must have people who are willing to listen to them. If no one had listened to Sanballat, the criticism would have died on the vine. But we love to listen to criticism, don't we? We would much rather listen to a negative statement about someone and spread that around, than listen to a positive, affirming statement and pass that around. That is why critics flourish. If you wish to avoid being dragged through the slime of criticism, if you want to avoid becoming a career critic. . .then you cannot run with critics.

The fourth identifying mark of critics and their criticism is that *criticism encourages exaggeration and sarcasm.* Back up in our text to verse 2 one more time.

Sanballat asked a series of sarcastic and exaggerated questions. *"What are these feeble Jews doing? Are they going to restore it for themselves? Can they offer sacrifices? Can they finish in a day? Can they revive the stones from the dusty rubble even the burned ones?"* And he attacks the character of the people—"What are these *feeble* Jews doing?" The word *feeble* is used here in the sense of "frail, miserable, withered, and powerless." The implication is, "How in the world could *they* do anything worthwhile."

Sanballat, in his mocking, follows a pattern of opposition which has been used throughout history. He begins with contempt for the people. Through his disdain he attempts to lower their self-esteem, weaken their resolve, and destroy their morale.

We have all met people like Sanballat. They delight in putting others down. Their scornful words put us on the defensive and take the joy out of what we are doing. They say things like, *"Who do you think you are, anyway?"* or, *"You don't know what you're talking about, you're just a. . . ."* This list of opening gambits is endless. . .but it zeroes in on your character. Dr. Maurice Wagner explains what happens when critics approach us this way. Listen:

Hostility, expressed in criticism. . .makes us relate to others without actually relating. A contact is made, but not to be helpful—all the critic is interested in is finding fault. We usually attack the person's self-esteem in ways he is totally helpless to correct. We label him as stupid, foolish, bad, ugly, ridiculous, etc. The critic shows no interest in the person's improvement; he is satisfied with being critical. [6]

But the exaggeration and sarcasm don't stop there. Sanballat exaggerates his statements to imply that the job was too big for them and that they will never be able to complete the project. They had tried before and met with failure. . .this time is no different.

When you are a critic. . .exaggeration is a favorite tactic. After all, the truth won't work. . .people won't listen to that. . . so stretch it a bit. . .mix it with sarcasm and you're in business. We do it all the time. You've done it. . . .I've done it. Dr. Joe Stowell, president of Moody Bible Institute, in his book *Tongue in Check* states:

Exaggeration is nothing more than lying about details to make information more sensational, interesting or manipulative. Exaggeration erodes trust and credibility, two building blocks of successful relationships. If you are given to critical exaggeration...don't be surprised when you wake up one day and find you have no real friends. [7]

Criticism that encourages exaggeration and sarcasm attacks the character of people; it attempts to magnify their problems. And if those approaches do not make much headway, criticism will attack, not just what you hope to do, but what you are presently doing. Tobiah the Ammonite did that. He mocked their efforts by saying, "If a fox jumped up on it, he would break

59

their stone wall down!"

People given to sarcasm are often very proficient with their criticism. *Webster's New Collegiate Dictionary* defines sarcasm as, *"A sharp and often satirical or ironic utterance designed to cut or give pain. . .a mode of satirical wit depending for its effect on bitter, caustic. . .language that is usually directed against an individual."*

From such dimly lit alleys, the critic attacks. If you have recently been on the receiving end of these kinds of tactics, then you know the deep agony of heart that unjustified criticism produces. The issue of how to handle it then becomes important. And there are a variety of approaches. I like the suggestion of Dr. R.C. Sproul. He writes:

> *I live a public life, a public ministry, write books and I get letters all the time and they just rake me up one side and down the other. I think people must sit up at nights thinking up ways to devastate me. I talked to another person in public ministry about it and asked him: "Do you ever get any hate mail?" He replied, "I get it all the time," "Well, how do you handle it," I asked. He said, "I write these people back and say, 'Dear Mr. So and So: I want to warn you about something dreadful. Some lunatic is sending me outrageous letters and signing your name to them.'"* [8]

That's one approach. Nehemiah had another. *"Hear us, O our God, for we are despised. Turn their insults back on their own heads. Give them over as plunder in a land of captivity. Do not cover up their guilt or blot out their sins from your sight, for they have thrown insults in the face of the builders. . . .But we prayed to our God. . . (4:4-5, 9a).*

Nehemiah dealt with the criticism through prayer. Through the practical resource of time on his knees, Nehemiah laid out his concerns before God. In prayer, Nehemiah is able to give full expression to his feelings. He does not suppress his emotions or bottle up his frustration and anger inside of him. He tells the Lord exactly how he feels—and that this isn't just a prayer for personal vindication. He says, "they have thrown insults in the face of the builders." Not "in my face."

It's okay to let God know how you're feeling. He knows anyway, but there is great value in talking to Him about it because criticism takes its toll. It's strange how words can crush us. Try to weigh a word and you'll find it hard to catch, much less weigh. How clever of our critics to attack us with words which vanish—into the throbbing flesh of our hearts and minds.

Nehemiah had a deep sense of God's purposes at work. . .so that criticism was not seen simply in human terms, but as opposition to God Himself. Nehemiah saw the Jews' enemies as God's enemies and His honor being compromised in this attack on His people. So Nehemiah cries out for justice. He places his appeal in the court of heaven, before the Almighty Judge. Just like some of us have, but don't want to admit to it.

Nehemiah began to deal with the blows of criticism by honestly confessing his despair and his hurt and his anger to his God. That's the first step. . .*prayer*.

The second is that we must simply go on. . .we *must persevere*. When Nehemiah and his fellow laborers joined together, it was not a half-hearted, easily defeated effort, for the people "worked with all their heart" (4:6).

Everyone pitched in—from the high priest, to the gold-smiths, the perfume makers, and the women. Everyone did something to help with the project. They hung in there. Why? Because they *"had the heart to work."* Their attitude carried the day. Nehemiah did not allow the lack of participation of one small group (the nobles of Tekoa) nor the vocal barrage of the critics to stop the project. He knew that the vast majority of the people were with him. . .and so they persevered. He did not argue with the critics. He did not defend himself publicly. What he did was finish the task.

There is one other part to handling criticism. Not only did he pray and persevere, he remained *very practical.*

But we prayed to our God, and because of them we set up a guard against them day and night.

To have only prayed would have been presumptuous and to have only set a guard would have indicated a lack of faith. Nehemiah shows us a wonderful balance. He was realistic enough to know that he couldn't relax. . .he couldn't let his guard down. . .he couldn't pretend that the attacks would simply stop because he prayed and persevered. Nehemiah stayed practical. He put a guard up on the wall.

When the guns of the enemy are directed your way, remember: You can never escape disapproval, regardless of how much you may want it to go away.

FOOTNOTES:
[1]"Conversations at the White House" from Frances B. Carpenter's six months at the White House with Abe Lincoln 1866. Cited in *Bartlett's Familiar Quotations* by John Bartlett, 14th edition, (Little, Brown & Co., Boston, MA, 1968), p. 641.

[2]Robert D. Foster, *The Navigator,* (NavPress, Colorado Springs, CO, 1983), p. 17.

[3]Donald K. Campbell, *Nehemiah: Man in Charge,* (Victor Books, Wheaton, IL, 1979), p. 35.

[4]David Augsberger, *The Freedom of Forgiveness,* (Moody Press, Chicago, IL, 1970), pp. 33-34.

[5]John Edward Lantz, *Speaking in the Church*, (MacMillan, New York, NY, 1964), p. 108.

[6]Maurice Wagner, *Put It All Together,* (Zondervan Corporation, Grand Rapids, MI, 1974), p. 131.

[7]Joseph M. Stowell, *Tongue in Check,* (Victor Books, Wheaton, IL, 1983), p. 51.

[8]R.C. Sproul, The Sanctity of Life Conference, June 1987, p. 6.

CHAPTER FIVE

WHEN CRITICISM WON'T STOP
(Nehemiah 4:10-23)

When criticism hounds your steps. . .when innuendo and rumor, like ocean breakers, roll unabated across your life. . . it takes its toll, doesn't it? It did for Nehemiah and his friends in the city of Jerusalem some 2,400 years ago. It was intense—and it didn't let up. In fact, details of those difficult days *when criticism wouldn't stop* reveal for us the all too painful effects that criticism has on our hearts.

The first of those effects is *discouragement*. Listen to the discouragement in Nehemiah's prayer that emerges out of the first wave of criticism.

"Hear, O our God, how we are despised! Return their reproach on their own heads and give them up for plunder in a land of captivity. Do not forgive their iniquity and let not their sin be blotted out before Thee, for they have de-moralized the builders."(Nehemiah 4:4-5)

The word despised comes from a verb that means *"to view someone as insignificant, to despise that one to the point of rejecting them."* Nehemiah looks to heaven and cries, *"Lord, see how we have been rejected. We are seen as insignificant, as useless, as unimportant, Lord. . .and it hurts."*

That's how criticism makes you feel: worthless. You feel like you can't do anything right anymore. . .you feel discouraged.

Do you feel that way right now? Your spouse will not let up. The boss's constant nitpicking has left you feeling like you are not worth a thing. Friends may have turned on you. Peers seem to have only one apparent joy in life—to demoralize you by never ending verbal assaults. You understand discouragement.

That is one of the first effects of unrelenting criticism. The second follows closely on its heels—*a sense of weariness* overcomes you. It happened to the rebuilders of Jerusalem's walls. After the initial rush of criticism from their enemies...the threat did not end, and the people who were working on the rebuilding project began to stumble and stagger from weakness and weariness. The wall has been completed to half its height, according to Nehemiah 4:6. Initially, despite the criticism, morale is high. Unfortunately, under renewed pressure, the enthusiasm of the people begins to fade. By verse 10, discouragement sets in and with it, a weariness of heart. The criticism continues, but they can't.

Thus in Judah it was said, "The strength of the burden bearers is failing, yet there is much rubbish; and we ourselves are unable to rebuild the wall" (4:10).

Solomon understood that kind of pressure. In Proverbs 4:16, he writes of those who attack us: *"...they cannot sleep unless they do evil; and they are robbed of sleep unless they make someone stumble."*

That kind of oppression wearies you. What you normally could have handled or rebounded from now becomes infinitely more difficult because you're too tired to go on. The Apostle Paul understood that kind of weariness. In II Corinthians 1:8 he wrote:

We do not want you to be unaware, brethren, of our affliction which came to us in Asia, that we were burdened excessively, beyond our strength, so that we despaired even of life.

Can you hear Paul saying that it was all almost too much for him? I can. All of the trials, the beatings, the imprisonments, and persecution weighed on him. He became depressed . . .weary.

We can only go for so long in the face of unrelenting opposition until our spirit cries, "Enough! I can't take anymore."

We view the heroes of faith wrongly if we imagine they never faced the same feelings you and I do. Our hurts, humiliations, and heartaches are part of the fabric of the lives of every Christian, every ordinary hero, every child of God.

Our moments of weakness, hurt, and weariness are often the terrible effects of criticism on our heart.

There is a third effect. Not only are we discouraged—and *so* tired—we become *defeated.*

Thus in Judah it was said, "The strength of the burden bearers is failing, yet there is much rubbish; And we ourselves are unable to rebuild the wall (4:10).

This, of course, is descriptive of the debris that lay scattered around the ruined city of Jerusalem. It had been there from the start. They'd lived in and around it for 150 years. But now it's different. . .because of the criticism. Now the piles of rubble have grown in their minds to become large and forbidding obstacles. So the people come to Nehemiah and lament: *"Nehemiah, all we can see is debris—dirt, broken stones, hard, dried chunks of mortar. It's getting tiring. There's too much rubbish. We can't do this."*

The builders had lost the vision of the completed wall. But that is precisely what happens to us when criticism keeps coming. What has been accomplished is forgotten; what can be accomplished is lost sight of. . .because all we see is the *"rubbish"* of the moment.

September 27, 1914 marked the tenth anniversary of Dr. G. Campbell Morgan as senior pastor of the Westminster Chapel in London. As he read his text of the morning, the congregation waited, wondering what he had in his heart to say to them. All they were aware of was the strangeness of the things he was saying, of how perplexed and troubled he was. The man who had literally lifted a derelict church up and set it on a pinnacle was telling his people that, could he have foreseen the disappointments and disillusionments in store for him years earlier, he would never have dared to come. These are his words that morning:

"During these ten years I have known more of visions fading into mirages, or purposes failing (to be) fulfilled, of things of strength crumbling away in weakness than ever in my life before." [1]

Not apostles, not preachers, not the ordinary Christians of life are exempt. When you are the target of critics. . .and the pain is intense and the wounds are deep. . .you lose your vision. Problems that earlier you could have handled routinely, now grow out of proportion. Suddenly, they become impossibilities as the ghost of failure begins to haunt you. The words *"I am not able"* begin to control you. *"I can't do it,"* becomes a theme in minor key. An exaggerated sense of your own inadequacies begins to stifle you. As a mother, you doubt your ability to ever raise your children properly. . .as a husband, you are convinced that you've blown it for good. . . .If you are single, then the rubbish of your life shouts, *"You're no good; you're worthless";* the student cries, *"I am all alone, there is no one to be my friend. . .I will never make it."* Whatever debris there is in your life. . .when you are criticized routinely. . .you can see nothing else.

And when we come to that place, we easily slide under the influence of another effect of criticism. . .*we become afraid of the future.*

Nehemiah's enemies watched from a distance for the response of the Jews. Several commentators suggest that the people were so distraught that the words of Nehemiah 4:10

were actually sung by them, as a sort of dirge. Their enemies did not miss that. This was the right moment for them to spread fresh rumors and to dishearten them so that the whole project would go under. When they sensed a weak spot, they dug the verbal knives in a little further.

And our enemies said, "They will not know or see until we come among them, kill them, and put a stop to the work."

...The Jews who lived near them came and told us ten times, "They will come up against us from every place where you may turn" (4:11-12).

Sanballat is no fool. He targets the workers who lived outside the city of Jerusalem, those who lived in his territory. And he started a whispering campaign among them: *"We're going to slip into your so called city and kill you all before you know what has happened."*

Sanballat and his crew are spreading demoralizing doubts, and the tactic worked. They intended to graft fear into the hearts of the people and they did. The people came to Nehemiah in a state of panic. They kept repeating their fears...over and over.

Generally, for us, it is the unknown, the unexpected that produces the greatest panic. It is in the grip of fear that most of us freeze, unable to cope with the circumstances and complexities of life. We feel overwhelmed. Our view of Christ and the working of the Holy Spirit is temporarily obscured.

But that is what the critic wants to have happen. People who traffic in criticism keep pouring it on. They look for a letdown from you, a weakness, a chink in the armor, an indication that they are getting to you, and then they move in...hoping to infect you with fear.

When we are afraid, defeated, weary, and discouraged, we echo the words we should know by heart by now, from the pen of an unknown author who writes:

"Lord, this soldier is tired, so very tired. He's worn to

the bone from the battle: never a cease-fire. So very tired.

Nothing makes sense, Lord; everything's so wrong. The battle he's fought has defeated him—(and yet) the battle's not over.

Beyond the defeat a ray of hope lies, faint, so very faint, but there. The hope to go on and win.

Lord, watch over this soldier. Pick him up, brush him off, show him you understand and care. Bless this soldier, Lord, 'cause he's me."

When you are a tired soldier, and the battle won't stop, where is that ray of hope. . .where is it? In the same four places that Nehemiah and his friends found it as they stumbled across the antidotes for criticism and the hope to go on.

That first antidote is hidden in Nehemiah 4:13.

Then I stationed men in the lowest parts of the space behind the wall, the exposed places, and I stationed the people in families with their swords, spears, and bows.

Nehemiah responds to the threat of attack by stopping the work and mobilizing the people as a show of strength to the enemy. He organizes them into defensive units. His tactic is to arm the people and station them in visibly strategic places along the wall. But don't miss the fact that he grouped the people together in families. He doesn't put Dad down at one end, Mom somewhere else, and the kids in yet another place. He brings them together because he knows that there is strength in the family. Standing beside one another, standing together. . . Nehemiah knew they would find encouragement and courage. He knew there would be an arm around the shoulder when the shoulders drooped. . .an embrace and a kiss when the pain was the worst. . .a soft hand to the cheek when the tears flowed. When we are under attack, when criticism assaults our spirit. . . *a close family* can help.

If you are single, you still have a family somewhere, a church family, a family of friends (Psalm 68:6 and Ephesians 3:14-15).

All of us have families. Do you find strength from your family? Do you look to them for encouragement when the artillery of the enemy is the most intense? Does your home provide you with a needed place of refuge? It should. If ever there should be a place where constant, unjustified criticism is rare, it is in our families.

Bob Benson has caught it. In his delightful book, *Laughter in the Walls*, he talks about the value of a close family.

I pass a lot of houses on my way home—some pretty, some expensive, some inviting—but my heart always skips a beat when I turn down the road and see my house nestled against the hill. I guess I'm especially proud of the house and the way it looks because I drew the plans myself. It started out large enough for us—I even had a study—two teenaged boys now reside there. And it had a guest room— my girl and nine dolls are permanent guests. It had a small room Peg had hoped would be her sewing room—the two boys swinging on the dutch door have claimed this room as their own. So it really doesn't look right now as if I'm much of an architect. But it will get larger again—one by one they will go away to work, to college, to service, to their own houses, and then there will be room—a guest room, a study, and sewing room for just the two of us. But it won't be empty—every room, every nick in the coffee table will be crowded with memories. Memories of picnics, parties, Christmases, bedside vigils, summers, fires, winters, going barefoot, leaving for vacation, cats, conversations, black eyes, graduations, first dates, ball games, arguments, washing dishes, bicycles, dogs, boat rides, getting home from vacation, meals, rabbits, and a thousand other things that fill the lives of those who would raise five. And Peg and I will sit quietly by the fire and listen to the laughter in the walls. [2]

When the tears of life start to flow, because the criticism just won't stop, gather strength and joy from your family. But also from God, who consistently remains faithful to us. That's in Nehemiah 4:14:

When I saw their fear, I rose and spoke to the nobles, the officials, and the rest of the people: "Do not be afraid of them; remember the Lord who is great and awesome, and fight for your brothers, your sons, your daughters, your wives, and your houses."

For Nehemiah this was a time of crisis: his enemies were angry and critical of the Jews, and his own people were frightened by the continuous onslaught of the enemy. But Nehemiah, as only he could do, drew the people's attention to their real strength—their great God. He gave them a battle cry, *"Remember the Lord!!"* Nehemiah said to his people, *"You've got your eyes on rubbish, the debris, your own individual work. Get your eyes on the Lord. . . .He is faithful."*

As an antidote to criticism and its effects, we need friends who, in those times of crisis and criticism, will gently walk us through God's faithfulness in our lives. Take a personal inventory. Go back five years and write down everything that has come into your life of major proportion—the good and the bad. And then, beside each one, write down how the faithfulness of your *"great and awesome"* God assisted you in those times. That is what Nehemiah did for his people.

But beyond even that, he did something else for them. He provided them with a *rallying point.* God's Word records for us that:

As for the builders, each wore his sword girded at his side as he built, while the trumpeter stood near me. And I said to the nobles, the officials, and the rest of the people, "The work is great and extensive, and we are separated on the wall far from one another. At whatever place you hear the sound of the trumpet, rally to us there. Our God will fight for us" (4:18-20).

Sanballat and company had not attacked the city—yet—but Nehemiah wasn't about to be caught off guard. . .so he maintained the guard. But more than that, an alarm system was instituted. If there was an emergency at some spot on the wall, the trumpet would be sounded, and reinforcements would quickly gather at the point of attack.

When you are under attack, where can you run to, where is your rallying point? When someone sounds the trumpet of personal need in their life, do you rally to them or do you ignore them? We all need a rallying point. We need a close friend, somebody we can attach ourselves to when the attack comes. We cannot fight alone.

Do you have that kind of friend? Someone you can open up to? Someone who will keep in confidence what you say, who will listen and not condemn you? Someone who will be with you *"on the wall?"* Do you have someone you can call and say, "Hey, I'm hurting. . .I need somebody to talk to." Are you that kind of friend to someone else? Can they rally to you?

Charles Hanson Towne touched an exposed nerve when he wrote:

Around the corner I have a friend, in this great city that has no end. Yet days go by and weeks rush on, and before I know it, a year is gone. . . .

And I never see my old friend's face. . .for life is a swift and terrible race. He knows I like him just as well as in the days when I rang his bell and he rang mine.

We were younger then, and now we are busy, tired men: tired with playing a foolish game, tired of trying to make a name.

"Tomorrow," I say, "I will call on Jim just to show that

I am thinking of him." But tomorrow comes—and tomorrow goes. And the distance between us grows and grows.

Around the corner—yet miles away. . . . "Here's a telegram, sir". . . . "Jim died today." And that's what we get and deserve in the end: Around the corner, a vanished friend.[3]

When we are reeling from the laser-like blasts of the critics, it is important to enjoy the strength of a close family, the consistency of our faithful God, and the security of a rallying point.

But there is one final antidote. Unlike the first three, which focus on the help that is available to us from others, this antidote focuses on what *we* can do. . .how our service for others can help ease the personal load we feel. The fourth antidote—*a servant's heart.*

And it came about from that day on, that half of my servants carried on the work while half of them held the spears, the shields, the bows, and the breastplates; and the captains were behind the whole house of Judah. Those who were rebuilding the wall and those who carried burdens took their load with one hand doing the work and the other holding a weapon (4:16-17).

Everybody becomes involved here. Nehemiah's servants, who came with him from Persia, were like a private army, and they were armed for the battle. But there were only a small number of them, so those who carried the supplies—the burden bearers—were also drawn in. They carried a weapon in one hand and steadied the load on their heads with the other hand. Then, the main group of builders who needed both hands to work, strapped a weapon around their waists, just in case. And they didn't have 9-5 jobs (4:21-23). They worked from dawn until the stars appeared. Then they stayed inside the city all night so they could serve as guards.

Nighttime security had to be strengthened, so everybody worked overtime, well into the night. They didn't even take time to grab a shower. . .because they didn't want to run the risk of letting the others down.

One of the antidotes to the negative effects of criticism is a willingness to serve others. . .to overlook our situation in order to help in theirs. That is part of what is happening here. But there is something else.

At that time I also said to the people, "Let each man with his servant spend the night within Jerusalem so that they may be a guard for us by night and a laborer by day" (4:22).

The workers who lived outside the city were asked to remain in the city rather than return to their homes in suburbia. Part of the reason for that was so that they could help fight. But, additionally, Nehemiah knew that he had to remove them from the context of criticism if they were going to be able to serve effectively.

As Charles Swindoll observed in his book, *Hand Me Another Brick:*

You cannot constantly hear criticism and negativism without having some of it rub off on you. If you are prone to discouragement, you can't run the risk of spending a lot of your time with people who traffic in discouraging and (critical) information. [4]

Nehemiah understood that. So he took his friends out of the environment of criticism and surrounded them with positive friends, with family, and with the ever-present sense of God's presence.

Sometimes we have to do that. We have to associate with those who will encourage us, those who are on our side. . .in our corner. And as we do, we find it easier to concentrate on ministering to them in their time of need. If you had lived in the era of Nehemiah, how would he have viewed you? Would he have encouraged people to stay clear of you, because of your critical attacks? Or would he be able to say to someone, "Stick with them. They'll encourage you, they'll strengthen you. . . they'll help you serve."

FOOTNOTES:

[1]Jill Morgan, *A Man of the Word, The Life of G. Campbell Morgan,* (Fleming H. Revell Company, Old Tappan, NJ, 1951), p. 207.

[2]Bob Benson, *Laughter in the Walls,* (Impact Books, Nashville, TN, 1969), pp. 16-17. Used with permission.

[3]"Around the Corner" from *Selected Poems of Charles Hanson Towne.* Copyright, 1925, by D. Appleton & Company. Copyright renewal by Ara Searle. Reprinted by permission of the publisher, Dutton, an imprint of New American Library, a division of Penguin Books U.S.A., Inc.

[4]Charles R. Swindoll, *Hand Me Another Brick,* (Thomas Nelson Publishers, Nashville, TN, 1978), p. 84. Used with permission.

CHAPTER SIX

COURAGE AND CONFRONTATION
(Nehemiah 5:1-13)

Dr. James Dobson, in his book *Straight Talk to Men and Their Wives*, shares a story about a ten-year-old boy named Robert. He happened to be a patient of a physician who was a close friend. Because this boy was obnoxious, his visits were dreaded by the office staff. His passive mother watched in bewilderment each time he tore around the office grabbing everything in sight. During one visit, the physician observed some cavities in Robert's teeth and referred him to a dentist. Knowing that such a referral could end a professional relationship, he carefully selected an older dentist who reportedly understood children. The confrontation that followed now stands as one of the classic moments in the history of human conflict. This is the rest of Dr. Dobson's story:

Robert arrived in the dental office prepared for battle. "Get in the chair, young man," said the doctor. "No chance!" replied the boy. "Son, I told you to climb onto that chair, and that's what I intend for you to do," said the dentist. Robert stared at his opponent for a moment and then replied, "If you make me get in that chair, I will take off all my clothes." The dentist calmly said, "Son, take 'em off."

The boy forthwith removed his shirt, undershirt, shoes and socks and then looked up in defiance. "All right, son," said the dentist, "Now get in the chair."

"You didn't hear me," sputtered Robert, "I said if you make me get on that chair, I will take off all my clothes."

"Son, TAKE 'EM OFF," replied the man.

Robert proceeded to remove his pants and shorts, standing totally naked before the dentist and his assistant. "Now, son, get in the chair," said the doctor. Robert did as he was told and sat cooperatively through the entire procedure. When the cavities were drilled and filled, he was instructed to step down from the chair.

"Give me my clothes now," said the boy.

"I'm sorry," replied the dentist. "Tell your mother that we're going to keep your clothes tonight. She can pick them up tomorrow."

Can you comprehend the shock Robert's mother received when the door to the waiting room opened and there stood her son, as naked as the day he was born? The room was filled with patients, but Robert and his mom walked past them into the hall. They went down a public elevator and into the parking lot, ignoring the snickers of onlookers.

The next day, Robert's mother returned to retrieve his clothes and asked to have a word with the dentist. However, she did not come to protest. These were her sentiments: "You don't know how much I appreciate what happened here yesterday. You see, Robert has been blackmailing me about his clothes for years. Whenever we are in a public place, such as a grocery store, he makes unreasonable demands of me. If I don't immediately buy him what he wants, he threatens to take off all his clothes. YOU ARE THE FIRST PERSON TO CALL HIS BLUFF, doctor, and the impact on Robert has been incredible!" [1]

Nehemiah would have applauded that dentist because they were cut from the same bolt. They knew how to assess a problem and deal with it courageously. Perhaps that is no more clearly seen than in Nehemiah's experience in the fifth chapter of this story.

The enemies of the Jews and the reconstruction of the city of Jerusalem fade into the background to reveal a more subtle, but serious problem. We now discover a new threat. . .coming from *within*. And this problem is potentially more dangerous because it strikes at the peoples' most precious asset—their unity. All the time that the rebuilding of the city walls was taking place. . .behind the scenes, away from the blueprints, the cement and mortar. . .lurked a far deadlier enemy—the people themselves. And Nehemiah became the man to resolve the problem.

But notice how it came to his attention: *"Now there was a great outcry of the people and of their wives against their Jewish brothers" (5:1).*

The words *"a great outcry"* refer to a cry of distress. Originally, these words were descriptive of the sound of thunder. . .but they came to be used of the storms of life. And when used in that way—when the storm is beating down upon you—the words mean *"a call for help when under great distress."*

Nehemiah's people were crying out to him for help. They were in serious trouble. Their problems were so serious that even the wives joined in . And that is very unusual because in Nehemiah's day the women stayed very much in the shadows. But not here. . .because the problems they faced were literally of life and death intensity.

". . .Let us get grain that we may eat and live." And there were others who said, "We are mortgaging our fields, our vineyards, and our houses that we might get grain because of the famine" (5:2-3).

Their cry for help is based on legitimate, valid needs. It was not prompted by selfishness, greed, discontent, or jealousy.

They had real needs.

Many times we cry about things that we have no business crying about. We complain because our kids don't dress as sharply as someone else's or our furniture/home decorating isn't new, or we can't enjoy the same kinds of vacations as others, and on and on we go. Now, certainly, those are concerns to us, but they are not real needs.

The people described in Nehemiah 5:2 owned no property, no real estate. They were apartment dwellers, renters we might say. Whatever savings or resources they did have were used up while they worked on the walls. Now they have no money to buy food. Those who still had property were mortgaging it to get enough cash together to feed their families. And because of famine conditions at the time, it didn't look like they would recoup any of their losses in the near future.

All of that spells disaster for these people. A Jew had a strong attachment to family property and would give it up only if survival were at stake. And it was (5:4-5). Inflation was running around 50%, but they still had to pay taxes to the Persian government. So some had borrowed money to pay the king's taxes. The hope was that they could pay back the money they borrowed, but they had no crops or other resources left. When they could not pay back the money to the lenders. . .they sold their children into slavery. The children of the man in debt were taken into the service of the creditors and had to work for him until the debts were paid.

That's a tough, painful spot to be in, but the worst part of it all was that the complaints of the people were directed against "their Jewish brothers."

Why? Because it was the wealthy Jews of Jerusalem who were using this economic crunch to their advantage. They were the ones loaning money at exorbitant rates of interest. They were the ones foreclosing on properties. They were the ones who were taking their neighbors' children as slaves.

They were exploiting the poor, essentially out of their own greed. Their mindset on life was one of covetousness. They saw an opportunity. . .they exploited it. They moved in like sharks, and it didn't matter that these were their own people as long as they got what they wanted. Tim Kimmel, in his book *Little House on the Freeway,* comments that: *"Coveting is material inebriation. It's an addiction to things that don't last and a craving for things that don't really matter. It forces us to depend on tomorrow to bring us the happiness that today couldn't supply."* [2]

That's where these wealthy men were. The first and most common face greed wears is the mask of money, money, money. Greed is an excessive motivation to have more money. We see it all around us. Most people you meet in the workplace want more money for what they are doing. Most are woefully discontented with their salary. When that happens, the next step is easy. You tend to use people and love things. You tend to walk over and through people on your way to serving yourself.

That is precisely what had happened in Nehemiah 5. Reduced to the point of despair, the pressured people simply laid it out before Nehemiah. *"Look, we can't take it anymore. Why should the rich profit from our troubles, especially since we are brethren? We are giving up everything for Jerusalem."* Nehemiah now faced the most severe test of his leadership—internal division.

The easiest thing for him to do was to ignore the complaints. Just sort of sweep them under the rug and pretend that everything is great. But that is not Nehemiah.

He is going to deal with it. You see, he didn't listen to the likes of Sanballat and Tobiah. They did not traffic in truth, only innuendo. But he listens to these people. He was prepared to stop and listen to legitimate complaints because he knew from long experience that people who are deeply concerned over some personal misfortune or problem cannot give their best to anything.

More than that, he knew that disunity ignored within the ranks would do more damage than Sanballat and his cronies.

The late Thom Hopler tells an interesting story.

When I first held tryouts in Kenya for a track meet, I could not get the students to compete against each other. They said, "We will select the one who is the fastest runner. He will run against the other school." I asked, "Why do that?" They said, "If we pick the one who can run best for us, then we can all cheer him on to victory against the other school. But we could never cheer him on to victory if he had selected himself by his own qualities. If we compete against ourselves, WE WILL DIVIDE OUR-SELVES, and we will not be able to compete against the other school." [3]

Nehemiah understood the importance of unity on his team, so he made the decision to act. The first thing Nehemiah did was admit he was angry (5:6). He did not excuse it, ignore it, or minimize it. He did not try to project it on others or blame them for the way he felt. He didn't try to repress it. He says, to translate loosely, that he's ticked off.

What the ridicule and criticism of the enemies had failed to do, the greed and exploitation of the wealthy Jews had accomplished. The opposition from the outside was expected, but not this disruption from his own people—and Nehemiah was incensed. Nehemiah knew that the laws of Moses forbade what was going on here. These men were in violation of God's Word and that made him very angry.

In *The Temptation To Be Good,* the author wrote: *"That is one of the serious things that has happened to the multitude of ordinary people. They have forgotten how to be indignant. This is because they are morally soft. When they see evil, they mutter and mumble; they never cry out. They commit the sin of not being angry."* [4]

Do you ever get angry at injustice. . .at sin, at clear violations of the Word of God? Instead of smiling smugly at blatant sin, do you ever utter a "holy snarl?"

Nehemiah was angry. But he did a very wise thing with his anger. According to Nehemiah 5:7, he talked to himself. I don't know what he said. Maybe he said, "Nehemiah. . .be careful, you're getting upset. . .count to 10!" He didn't jump into action, make snap judgments or do what so many of us do when we become angry—he didn't gossip about it. He pondered the charges in his mind. Avoiding the temptation of maligning others, he steered clear of inflammatory remarks.

Nehemiah knew the wisdom of deliberating before taking action. Hasty, knee-jerk reactions and quick judgments only intensify our problems. By giving himself time to analyze and evaluate the situation, Nehemiah avoided rash, impulsive actions that would have made things worse.

Columnist Louis Cassels has said that the hardest moral duty of our time is for men and women to keep on caring. We are exposed daily to so much human tragedy that we experience what someone has called *"compassion fatigue."* But even worse than compassion fatigue, said Cassels, is *"indignation fatigue."*

Many of us seem to have lost the capacity to get mad— or at least, as mad as we ought to get about lying, cheating, stealing. . . .To be indifferent to wrongdoing, to shrug it off or laugh at it, is a symptom of advanced degradation of the moral sense. Someone seems to have administered a massive dose of novocaine to our national conscience. [5]

Nehemiah was not afflicted with compassion fatigue or indignation fatigue. Nor was he a man who did nothing about things that were wrong. After he'd weighed the accusations, he faced the officials and nobles in private: "You are exacting usury from your own countrymen!" Then in a large meeting Nehemiah faced them in righteous anger and said, "Now you are selling your brothers, only for them to be sold back to us!" And the nobles could say nothing. The charge was true. So Nehemiah roars at them, "What you are doing is not right. Shouldn't you walk in the fear of our God to avoid the reproach of our Gentile enemies? I and my brothers and my men are also lending the people money and grain. But let the exacting of usury stop! Give back to them immediately their fields, vineyards, olive groves and houses, and also the usury you are charging them" (Nehemiah 5:6-11).

So often, we lack the courage to openly confront those who are in the wrong. Not Nehemiah. He confronts the nobles. He does not allow the problems to smolder indefinitely. He courageously faced and rebuked the guilty parties. And it wasn't a quiet time. The verb originally used indicates a noisy argument, even shouting took place. There are times for that. And this was one of them.

Nehemiah faced these men with determination, knowing that he must do what was right, letting the dust fall where it may. Nehemiah's charge was that they were *"exacting usury"* against the people. That means that they were lending money at high interest rates. The laws of the Old Testament sought to prevent that kind of abuse of people; therefore, interest bearing loans were forbidden between the Jews. In fact, after a certain period of time both loans and slaves were to be forgiven and freed because generosity was encouraged as the rule. On matters like these, the law appealed to the heart.

But these men had lost their heart and were treating their fellow Jews like commodities. Nehemiah wouldn't stand for it.

Nehemiah tells the nobles in private exactly what he thinks

of them. John White, in his commentary on Nehemiah, says, "Nehemiah does not allow himself to be weak. . . .Whatever their future relationships may prove to be, the nobles will say of Nehemiah, 'We may not agree with him, but at least we always know where he stands.' Godly leaders cannot afford to be two-faced. Our publicly and privately expressed views must coincide."[6]

Is that true of you? Or do you express one thing to one person or group and the opposite to another, just to be popular, just to be accepted, just so you don't rock the boat? Do you smile and tell one person that you think they are the greatest, and then behind their back accuse them of all sorts of things? Do you surrender your convictions just because someone with influence and power disagrees with you?

The easiest thing in the world for Nehemiah would have been to back down, to look the other way, to pretend nothing was wrong. After all, who wants to confront nobles and rulers? Who wants to go after the people of clout, the people who finance things? Nobody is that stupid. . .or maybe no one has enough courage.

Nehemiah wanted to remain morally right. . .so he went to these men privately. Apparently it had no effect on them, so Nehemiah was forced to bring the matter before all the people. These men seemed ready for a power struggle. The priests (who should have challenged their conduct) had long since been won over to their side and no one has come along recently to tell them that their business practices are contrary to the Word of God.

No one that is, until Nehemiah. In front of everybody Nehemiah calls them to account.

What was their response? "They kept quiet, because they could find nothing to say" (5:8).

They were speechless. They are shamed into silence. They

have no reply because they know in their heart of hearts that they are guilty. Would that have been our response? Or would we have attempted to justify our actions. . .or rationalize them away? Chuck Swindoll, as only he can, puts this in terms we can all come to grips with:

Correcting any problem begins by facing it head-on. Some of us are pros at avoiding the truth. Because it is painful to confront sin in our lives, we dodge it. We excuse it. In essence, we don't want to endure the pain of reality— and so we hide behind the famous cop-out: "Oh well, nobody's perfect. You know, that's just the way I am. Always have been—always will be." Who says? God is a specialist in the business of changing lives. Claim the power of the indwelling Holy Spirit and say, "God, take over. Change my attitude. I'm sick of this habit. It is sin." [7]

Whether it is an uncontrollable tongue that indulges in lying, gossip, exaggeration or criticism; a quick temper or drinking; a malicious spirit or apathy about the things of God, it is sin. And no matter how painful it is to acknowledge it, it is even more hurtful to continue to harbor it.

That's what Nehemiah has done. But conviction of sin and repentance of it does not stop at silence. Repentance includes a change of behavior; it includes repairing the damage if that is possible. There are always consequences to our wrong actions. Nehemiah understood that and that is why he demands that the wrongs be made right. And he seals it with a solemn promise before God.

I also shook out the front of my garment and said, "Thus may God shake out every man from his house and from his possessions who does not fulfill this promise; even thus may he be shaken out and emptied." And all the assembly said, "Amen!" And they praised the Lord. Then the people did according to this promise (5:13).

Nehemiah told the nobles: 1) stop lending money for profit; 2) give back the land, houses, and people on which they have foreclosed, and 3) return the interest money they had collected (verses 10-11).

Now, of course, they smiled and agreed. Just like that. These men are overwhelmed with Nehemiah's courage and so they're prepared to say anything. But Nehemiah was a realist. He knew how easy it is to fake repentance. We say we'll go along with something, but inwardly hope that when the smoke clears, no one will remember what we promised.

Nehemiah knew that route was all too easy. So he applied the screws a little tighter. He required a public promise to God. "So I called the priests and took an oath from them that they would do according to this promise" (5:12b).

Nehemiah called the priests in—the men who were supposed to represent the Jews to God. Pointing to the cutthroat money-lenders, he said, *"You men make a promise to these men over here. And, you priests, remember this before God."* It was a public hearing, a public declaration, and a public promise before God. Then to make sure they caught the significance, Nehemiah outlines the negative consequences if they renege on their promise in verse 13. He is saying, in effect, *"This is serious, folks. A vow to God is not something you shrug off."*

Or is it? How many of us have done precisely that? Caught in our sin, we repent, we make promises to other people and to God to clean up our life. . .to stop dividing the body. . .to operate ethically and honestly. . . to remain pure morally. . . to not be two-faced. We may even have made a public confession. But when the pressure eases. . .so does our resolve to change.

Perhaps you have been confronted about sin in your life. You admitted it, said you'd change. And you did. . . .This time you were more careful; you covered your tracks better. You're still it now. When we're confronted with our sin, how do we react?

Do we rant and rave about the audacity of people? Turn around and blame the people who approached us?

It is only *after* these people have come to terms with their sin. . .it is only *after* they have come to terms with God and what His Word says that they are able to move beyond their problems and worship Him. *"And all the assembly said, 'Amen!' And they praised the Lord. Then the people did according to this promise" (5:13).*

This great crowd of people, so close to splitting apart at the seams, now raises their voices to heaven, praising God that the problems have been resolved. Once divided, but now united. It is significant that it is only after they responded this way that the work on the city wall was completed. And nobody's bent out of shape with the correction or the confrontation; that's the amazing part. Nobody decides to leave Jerusalem. Nobody goes off in a huff. Instead, they are lifting their hearts and their voices in praise to their wonderful God. What a magnificent response! I wish I could remember a response like that in the church.

But the only reason they could do that was because they were beginning to take seriously the consequences of sin and their promise to God. In doing that, they were relieved from all the tension that had built up because of their sin. Free of that, they were able to worship. And the final statement of verse 13 indicates that the people had finally found joy in doing what was right in God's eyes.

Have we?

FOOTNOTES:
[1]James Dobson, *Straight Talk to Men and Their Wives*, (Word Books, Dallas, TX, 1980), pp. 58-60. Used with permission.

[2]Tim Kimmel, *Little House on the Freeway*, (Multnomah Press, Portland, OR, 1987), p. 119.

[3]John Stott, *Confess Your Sins: the Way of Reconciliation*, (Word, Inc., Dallas, TX, 1974), p. 49.

[4]A. Powell Davies, *The Temptation To Be Good,* (Beacon, Boston, MA, 1965), p. 119.

[5]Donald K. Campbell, *Nehemiah: Man in Charge,* (Victor Books, Wheaton, IL, 1979), pp. 47-48.

[6]John White, *Excellence in Leadership*, (InterVarsity Press, Downers Grove, IL, 1986), p. 82.

[7]Charles R. Swindoll, *Hand Me Another Brick,* (Thomas Nelson Publishers, Nashville, TN, 1978), pp. 109-110. Used with permission.

CHAPTER SEVEN

SERVANTHOOD: NEHEMIAH STYLE
(Nehemiah 5:14-19)

Her friends remember her as a warm, joyful, and vibrant person, as a woman of everlasting youth who loved amusement parks and French fries.

The rest of the world remembers her as a woman with flashing dark eyes and incomparable grace, as the greatest ballerina of all time. . .Anna Pavlova.

So deep was her sense of professional responsibility that she never missed a performance. Not once.

And yet, in one year alone, Anna gave 238 performances in 35 weeks, playing 77 towns and cities across the United States. In the course of her career, she travelled 500,000 miles, dancing before millions of people. . .and she did this before commercial air travel.

She performed everywhere so that all might enjoy her art. In Jackson, Mississippi, she danced in what amounted to an old garage. There was no stage, only a shallow platform. There were not even dressing rooms, just a few curtains hung in a cellar full of rats. And, yet, Anna performed there, as everywhere, cheerfully. It was as though life itself was so wonderful that there was no room for complaining.

In Montgomery, Alabama, there was a hole in the roof so large that rain poured in, flooding the stage, drenching the costumes and the scenery. Her only remark, after pirouetting through the puddles, was that the dancers needed no stage lights because of the lighting outside.

No, the great Anna Pavlova never missed a performance. It is perhaps because of her perfect record that her ardent admirers never forgot Anna's last scheduled appearance. It was to be at the Apollo Theater in London, in the role she made famous, the Dying Swan. In that particular role, Anna was known to have surpassed her own incredible technique and to have touched her audiences with the compassion of her interpretation.

It was in an atmosphere of unusual excitement that her fans awaited this farewell performance. On the appointed evening at the scheduled time the orchestra began, the curtain rose, the spotlight flashed—and the audience rose to its feet! All through the performance they stood, gazing into the wandering pool of light on the stage.

When it was finished, a raging, thunderous ovation of joy went up and on and on. Even though the spotlight had brushed across a totally empty stage throughout the entire performance.

For this was the ultimate tribute to the artistry of Anna Pavlova She had died two days before, having fallen ill with pneumonia. But even in her absence, her audience could see her.[1]

I rather feel that same way about Nehemiah. Even though he has long since bowed out of the spotlight. Even though he exited the stage of history centuries ago, his artistry lives on, and I sense that as we walk through the corridors of his life—as dusty as they may be—we, his audience, like Anna Pavlova's audience, can, even in his absence, still see him.

Alexander Maclaren, one of England's finest preachers during the last century, as he reflected on the artistry of Nehemiah, saw him this way:

Nehemiah. . .is one of the neglected great men of Scripture. He was no prophet, he had no glowing words, lofty visions, (nor) did he live in an heroic age. . . .But he was brave, cautious, and he had Jerusalem in his heart." [2]

"He had Jerusalem in his heart" is the crucial phrase in understanding Nehemiah. It was his love for his homeland, his people, and his God that drove him to take the courageous steps of leadership that he did. It would be easy, however, to lose sight of the fact that Nehemiah was motivated by a servant's heart. It would be easy to miss completely the real heartbeat of this man. It's revealed in the last several verses of Nehemiah 5. Following, as they do, on the heels of the courageous confrontation of sin by Nehemiah, they show that he was a servant.

But what makes that so remarkable is the position of prominence that Nehemiah held shortly after he arrived in Jerusalem. From the twentieth year of Artexerxes reign to the thirty-second year, Nehemiah was the king's appointed governor (5:14) in the land of Judah.

This was no *"oh by the way"* promotion either. It was a very prominent place to be in. It was a position of authority, of rank, of influence. . .where the values of a servant are easily lost.

In fact, the verb *"appointed"* literally means *"to be set in charge, to command someone (to do something), to send someone with orders, with a commission."* The term *"governor"* is a general administrative term used of a ruler who has been given great responsibility. Nehemiah had that kind of clout. But Nehemiah handled that kind of promotion well, because positions of prominence and influence were not what he lived for.

Nehemiah knew how to use his victory properly. When news of the problems in Jerusalem first reached Nehemiah months earlier, he did not see that as the chance of a lifetime to win fame and fortune. He did not leave Persia and come to Jerusalem to become the governor. When he decided to come to Jerusalem, his one thought was to stand for God and to help those who were in distress. Promotions, places of prominence and influence, were incidentals along the way. *That* is the heart attitude where servants must begin.

If you are in a position of prominence professionally, or maybe you just want to be, it is very easy to forget about servanthood. We tend to want to be noticed, to be applauded, to be spotlighted, to be heard. We tend to develop a certain aura around us that says to others, *"Look at me! Look at who I am! Pay attention to me; I am important. I can make you do anything I want."*

And yet it is extremely significant that almost five chapters of Nehemiah's story pass before we are alerted to the fact that he has been promoted to the position of governor. If we had been in his sandals, the first thing we would have done is update our resume and print new business cards. Not Nehemiah.

The late Joe Bayly wrote: *"Save me, God, from success. I fear it more than failure—which alerts me to my nature, limitations (and) destiny. I know that any success apart from Your Spirit is mere euphemism for failure."* [3]

Nehemiah did not allow a position of prominence to alter his basic approach to life. . .that of a servant.

In fact, he went out of his way to model *a posture of servanthood.* He carefully and consistently made decisions and took actions that prove that. But in Nehemiah 5:14-19 God records them for us clearly. Nehemiah calls time out, as it were, to publicly declare his motivations. That suggests to me that there were some in Jerusalem who were beginning to question them. It tells us that somewhere in the shadows of Nehemiah's life and role as governor there lurked those who formed conclusions and reached verdicts about him that were not true. So, Nehemiah offers the rest of the story, to set his leadership in perspective. To begin, he points out the first element of servanthood. . .*servanthood is not self-serving.*

. . .*For twelve years, neither I nor my kinsmen have eaten the governor's food allowance (5:14).*

The governor in that time was entitled to draw his salary from the taxation that he levied on behalf of the throne. A governor had the right to collect taxes not only for the central treasury of the government, but also for his own savings plan. But during a 12-year period, Nehemiah took none of the customary allowances from the people. He actually served for 12 years without pay. Don't ignore that. In today's money, Nehemiah could have earned $1,200 *per day*. But he passed on it. The text suggests that he even drew on his private resources to maintain his staff. Obviously, possessions were less important to him than the work of the Lord. He used his own resources rather than take taxes from the people.

When is the last time we did something without looking for cost reimbursements or for somebody else to pick up the tab? The principle that Nehemiah so ably models is that *there are times when we need to give up what is rightfully ours for the sake of others.*

How foreign that concept is to much of our society! Christopher Lasch, in the book, *The New Culture of Narcissism,* observed: *"...When therapists speak of the need for 'meaning' and 'love' they define love and meaning simply as the fulfillment of (your) emotional requirements. It hardly occurs to them...to encourage the (person) to subordinate his needs and interests to those of others, to someone or some cause or tradition outside himself. 'Love as self-sacrifice or self-abasement...strike the therapeutic sensibility as intolerably oppressive, offensive to common sense and injurious to personal health and well-being."* [4]

Allan Bloom, in his best-seller *Closing of the American Mind,* argues that modern psychology believes that selfishness is somehow good. He says that one of the great changes in thinking today is that a good man used to be the one who cares for others, now it is the man who cares exclusively for himself.

Selfishness is a kind of greediness. Like all greediness it contains an insatiability. And greed is a bottomless pit which exhausts a person in an endless effort to satisfy *his* needs without ever reaching satisfaction. The selfish person is always anxiously concerned with himself; the world is seen only through the filter of how this will benefit him. He is never satisfied, always driven by the fear of not getting enough, of missing something, of being deprived of something.

Nehemiah was not like that. He understood that servanthood is not self-serving. By the way, when is the last time we gave up our rights for the sake of someone else? When did we consciously stop and say: "No, although I deserve this, I'll pass for their sake. . .and I'll do so without complaint?" When is the last time we put someone else's needs before our own?

Servanthood is not self-serving. . .nor is it *unreasonable*. The previous governors of Judah had placed heavy financial and material burdens on the people.

But the former governors. . .laid burdens on the people and took from them bread and wine besides forty shekels of silver; even their servants domineered the people. But I did not do so because of the fear of God (5:15).

The word "burden" comes from a verb that means "to cause to struggle with difficulties." They imposed the burden of increased taxation, much of which went to line their own pockets, and they kept upping the amount every year. They grew increasingly less satisfied and demanded more.

How common that is!

In national surveys conducted at the beginning of the 1980s, 62 percent of Americans consistently rejected this statement: *"The ways things are today, the fewer possessions you own, the less you have to worry about and the better off you are."* Yet, a 54 percent majority expressed a desire, *"to own more things than I have now."* For the overwhelming majority of all

Americans, an important part of living the good life simply means *"more."* [5]

There is nothing wrong with making money or having nice things. But, it is so easy to move from that place to the point where we *must make more money, and instead of having nice things, they have us.* We succumb to the love of money (I Timothy 6:10).

Nehemiah was not opposed to wealth. . .obviously he was well-off himself. But he did not allow his wealth to turn him into someone who used people for his own purposes.

The honest prayer of Robert A. Raines drips, like an intravenous feeding, into my bloodstream and thoughts when I think about this. He prayed:

"I am like James and John, Lord. Lord, I size up other people in terms of what they can do for me, how they further my program, feed my ego, satisfy my needs, give me strategic advantage.

I exploit people, ostensibly for your sake, but really for my own sake. Lord, I turn to you to get the inside track and obtain special favors, your direction for my schemes, your power for my projects, your sanction for my ambitions, your blank check for whatever I want. I am like James and John. Change me, Lord. Make me a man who asks of you and others, what can I do for you?" [6]

That was the heartbeat of Nehemiah's leadership. He was not motivated by selfishness or a desire to be unreasonable. He didn't want anyone to fear him or his power. In fact, it was just the opposite. He was in Jerusalem on behalf of the people, as a servant who was prepared *to sacrifice for others.*

And I also applied myself to the work on this wall; we did not buy any land, and all my servants were gathered there for the work (5:16).

Nehemiah applied himself to the work on the wall. That tells us two things. First of all, it means he was involved in the construction project himself. Nehemiah seems to have kept on the move among the builders, directing, encouraging, and keeping watch for any dangers. The scope of the book suggests that he slept little and worked late to make sure the job was done. In other words, he ministered at great personal sacrifice.

Nehemiah understood that ministry would cost him something. But it went even deeper for him. Because he devoted himself to the work on this wall, it also indicates that he contributed financially toward the construction costs—at considerable personal expense. Remember, he had permission to buy supplies. How did he buy them? With his own money! He used his own personal resources for virtual strangers.

That is a refreshing, challenging lesson on this man's life and character. You see, if we aren't servants at heart, we don't get involved in the ministry beyond complaining about it, and we certainly don't support it financially. What about you? Do you model this third element of a servant's posture? Are you involved in the ministry of your church in a positive way? How do you serve? What about finances? Are you giving sacrificially to that ministry? Are you giving until it hurts?

Nehemiah's behavior as governor was guided by principles of servanthood rather than opportunism. Nehemiah 5:16 tells us that Nehemiah did not buy any land. That does not mean that real estate investment is inappropriate. It's a statement of where his heart is. Land values would have been very low when Nehemiah arrived on the scene, but as he stabilized things in Jerusalem, land values would go up. To have made money would have been simple. Yet Nehemiah refused to speculate. Not because it was wrong, but because he was not in Jerusalem to get, but to give. . .to sacrifice.

Think about that! Not only does he give up his rightful salary, but now he has a great chance to recoup some of his losses, and yet he refuses all such opportunities. Why? "But I did not do so because of the fear of God" (5:15). Nehemiah's motives came from the heart of a servant, and he wanted always to operate above board, with integrity, so that his every action honored the Lord God.

Do we operate that way? Burke Marketing Research, Inc. asked executives in 100 of the nation's 1,000 largest companies, "What employee behavior disturbs you the most?" According to the survey, these are the eight banes of a boss's existence. . .liars, goof-offs, egomaniacs, laggards, rebels, whiners, airheads, and sloths. But of those eight, lying or dishonesty topped the list. The conclusion of the research was summed up in this way: *If a company believes that an employee lacks integrity, all positive qualities, ranging from skill and experience to productivity and intelligence, become meaningless.*[7]

We won't behave as servants who are prepared to sacrifice for others if *integrity* is not high on our list of priorities. We will not be able to give up anything for anyone else.

There is one final posture of servanthood that Nehemiah so ably models—*servanthood is generous.*

Everyday Nehemiah fed 600-800 people (5:17-18). Why prepare food for 800?

The daily demands upon his generous hospitality were partly due to his political responsibilities as governor. That accounted for 200-300 of his guests. The rest of the people were there simply because of his generosity. They may have had no place else to go for food. They could have been the destitute, the homeless, widows, orphans, because no one needed a meal ticket to eat at Nehemiah's table. Nehemiah 5:18 tells us that he paid for all the food at his own expense. Anyone could come. No one was refused. Nehemiah understood the principle that when God blesses us with material things, we ought to share them with others. Even when people take advantage of you. Karen Burton Mains puts this into terms all of us can relate to:

Entertaining says, "I want to impress you with my home, my clever decorating, my cooking.' Hospitality, seeking to minister, says, "This home is a gift from my Master. I use it as He desires." Hospitality aims to serve. Entertaining puts things before people. "As soon as I get the house finished, the living room decorated, my house-cleaning done—then I will start inviting people. Hospital-ity puts people first. "No furniture—we'll eat on the floor!" "The decorating may never get done—you come anyway." "The house is a mess—but you are friends—come home with us." Entertaining subtly declares, "This home is mine, an expression of my personality. Look, please, and admire." Hospitality whispers, "What is mine is yours." [8]

Nehemiah behaved this way. Because he lived in the presence of God, everything he did was done out of an awareness of what was appropriate for one who worshipped and reverenced God. The verdict of heaven was very important to him. "Remember me, O my God, for good, according to all that I have done for this people" (5:19)

But there is a certain sadness in his voice here. It's as if he sensed that the people would soon forget or ignore his sacrificial service, so he prays that God will not. Ultimately, Nehemiah's goal was the approval of God, and he has done all these things not to receive the praise of people, but the smile of God.

Joseph Parker summarizes so well the character of Nehemiah:

Every act of his during his government speaks of one who had no selfishness in his nature. All he did was noble, high-minded, courageous, and to the highest degree, upright. And to stern integrity he united humility and kindness and a princely hospitality. But in nothing was he more remarkable than for his piety, and the singleness of eye with which he walked before God. He seems to have undertaken everything in dependence upon God, with prayer for His blessing and guidance and to have sought His reward only from God. [9]

Could that be said of us today? Do we point others to the bounty and magnificence of God by our actions without thought of "what's in it for me"?

FOOTNOTES:

[1]Paul Aurandt, *More of Paul Harvey's The Rest of the Story,* (William Morrow & Co. Inc, New York, NY, 1980), pp. 89-90. Used with permission.

[2]Alexander Maclaren, *Expositers of Holy Scripture,* (Baker Books, Grand Rapids, MI, 1984), Vol. 3, p. 361.

[3]Joseph Bayly, *Psalms of Life,* (David C. Cook Publishing Co., Elgin, IL, 1987), p. 16.

[4]Christopher Lasch, *The Culture of Narcissism,* (Warner Books, New York, NY, 1979), pp. 42-43.

[5]Daniel Yankelovich, *New Rules,* (Bantam Books, New York, NY, 1981), p. 174.

[6]Robert A. Raines, *Creative Brooding*, (MacMillan Publishing Co., Inc., New York, NY, 1966). Used with permission.

[7]Zig Ziglar, *Top Performance,* (Fleming H. Revell Company, Old Tappan, NJ, 1986), p. 103.

[8]Used with permission by David C. Cook Publishing Company, *Open Heart, Open Home*, by Karen Burton Mains. Copyright 1976.

[9]Joseph Parker, *The People's Bible: Discourses Upon Holy Scripture,* (Hazell, Watson & Viney, LD, London, England, 1889), Vol. X, p. 227.

CHAPTER EIGHT

WHEN INTIMIDATION COMES CALLING

(Nehemiah 6:1-19)

There were once two men, Mr. Wilson and Mr. Thompson, both seriously ill in the same room of a hospital. It was quite a small room, just large enough for the pair of them. One window looked out on the world.

Mr. Wilson, as part of his treatment, was allowed to sit up in bed for an hour in the afternoon. His bed was next to the window. But Mr. Thompson had to spend all of his time flat on his back. Both of them had to be kept quiet and still, which was the reason they were in the small room by themselves. They were grateful for the peace and privacy, though. There was none of the bustle and clatter and prying eyes of the general ward. Of course, one of the disadvantages of their condition was that they weren't allowed to do much: no reading, no radio, certainly no television. They just had to keep quiet and still.

So they used to talk for hours and hours. About their wives, their children, their homes, their jobs, their hobbies, their childhood, where they'd been on vacations, all that sort of thing. Every afternoon, when Mr. Wilson, the man by the window, was propped up for his hour, he would pass the time by describing what he could see outside. And Mr. Thompson began to live for those hours.

The window apparently overlooked a park with a lake where there were ducks and swans, children throwing them bread and sailing model boats, and young lovers walking hand in hand beneath the trees. And there were flowers and stretches of grass, games of softball, people taking their ease in the sunshine, and right at the back, behind the fringe of trees, there was a fine view of the city skyline. Mr. Thompson listened to all of this, enjoying every minute. How a child nearly fell into the lake, how beautiful the girls were in their summer dresses, then an exciting ball game, or a boy playing with his puppy. It got to the point that he could almost see what was happening outside.

Then one fine afternoon, when there was some sort of a parade, the thought struck him: Why should Wilson, next to the window, have all the pleasure of seeing what was going on? Why shouldn't *he* get the chance? He felt ashamed and tried not to think like that, but the more he tried, the worse he wanted a change. He would do anything! In a few days, he had turned sour. *He* should be by the window, he brooded. He couldn't sleep and grew even more seriously ill which the doctors just couldn't understand.

One night as he stared at the ceiling, Mr. Wilson suddenly woke up, coughing and choking, the fluid congesting in his lungs. His hands groped for the call button that would bring the night nurse running, but he couldn't reach it. Mr. Thompson watched without moving. The coughing racked the darkness. On and on. Mr. Wilson choked and then stopped. The sound of breathing stopped. Mr. Thompson continued to stare at the ceiling.

In the morning, the day nurse came in with water for their baths and found Mr. Wilson dead. They took his body away quietly, with no fuss.

As soon as it seemed decent, Mr. Thompson asked if he could be moved to the bed next to the window. So they moved him, tucked him in, made him quite comfortable, and left him alone. The minute they'd gone, he propped himself up on one elbow, painfully and laboriously, and strained as he looked out the window. . . . It faced a blank wall.

Significantly, as we wander through the corridors of the book of Nehemiah. . .as we encounter the memories of this great leader. . .what we do not find is the mention of a friend. Nowhere in the book. . .not even reading between the lines. . .is there a record of Nehemiah being supported, listened to, or assisted by a friend or wife. Instead, we find all too many references to Mr. Thompsons. The personal memoirs of Nehemiah describe a man who stood alone and betrayed. . .except by God. Often that is the path we have to take. It is a road we travel alone.

That is especially true *when intimidation comes calling.* We find out very quickly, when others oppose us and attempt to intimidate us, who our friends are. Frequently, we discover that we must face intimidation on our own. Just as Nehemiah did in the sixth chapter of his story. When that happens, it is helpful to know in advance some of *the tactics used by intimidators.*

The first tactic employed by those who would intimidate us is *intrigue.*

When Sanballat and his crew realize that they have been outmaneuvered, outgeneraled, and outwitted by Nehemiah, they decide to attack him personally. They launch a war of nerves against Nehemiah because they had finally come to see that he was the key to the entire project—remove him from the scene and the work would stop immediately (6:1-2).

By the way, if we are doing something of positive value and there are those who don't like what we we're doing, but can't seem to stop it. . .be ready for them. Sooner or later they will attack us personally. Unfortunately, that's as true of the church as it is in business, politics, or volunteer work.

Sanballat and friends invite Nehemiah to a summit conference of sorts, in a neutral location, some distance from Jerusalem, out in the country—where they can talk. They say, in effect, "Nehemiah, let's be friends. We've had our differences in the past, but we need to get along. So, let's meet together, resolve our differences and plan for peace."

They offered to meet Nehemiah under the pretence of reconciliation. And they didn't give up easily. They presented their plan to Nehemiah three more times. But the real purpose of the proposed conference was to lure Nehemiah away from Jerusalem to a place where his assassination would be easier. Those who would intimidate often begin with high sounding words... but with evil in their hearts. And Nehemiah saw through their subterfuge. He had seen enough of their actions in the past to see beyond their words now and know that they had not had a change of heart. With divine wisdom, he knew that if they were sincere, they would have met with him in Jerusalem, in public. The out-of-the way place, far from the city and his army escort, was an obvious trap.

The great reformers of the faith, John Huss and William Tyndale, both had experiences like this. Huss was invited to attend the Council of Constance in 1414 to answer charges against him. The emperor promised him safe conduct both ways. But he was seized and thrown into a dungeon, later to be condemned by that council and burned at the stake. Tyndale, the translator of the English Bible, was living in exile in Belgium when he was invited to have lunch with a supposed friend. It turned out to be a trap and he was arrested; several months later, in 1535, he was strangled and burned.

Intimidators enjoy the tactic of intrigue. But if that does not work, then tactic number two is the next step. . .*innuendo.*

Then Sanballat sent his servant to me in the same manner a fifth time with an open letter in his hand (6:5).

Letters during this time were written on a papyrus or leather sheet, rolled up, tied with a string and then sealed with a clay impression. That impression was to guarantee its confidentiality. But Sanballat obviously had something else in mind, because when Nehemiah refuses to walk into his trap, he puts some serious accusations in writing. The letter Nehemiah receives is unsealed. That means that the contents of the letter were intended for public consumption. Sanballat knows that by sending it unsealed, it will be read many times on its way to Jerusalem. And those reading it will be told: 1) that Nehemiah and the Jews were plotting treason against the Persian government; 2) that Nehemiah's goal was really to be king; and 3) that Nehemiah even bribed some enthusiastic prophets to support him in his drive to the throne.

The charge of treason, even if Nehemiah can prove that it is not true, will be sufficient to impugn Nehemiah's motives, cast doubts on his integrity, and undermine his influence. It might even reach the king and make him question Nehemiah's loyalty—a sure way to get him *permanently* removed. And this widely publicized letter will become a source of an ever widening circle of gossip and rumor that some people will believe.

That's because this attack on Nehemiah takes advantage of an important psychological principle—*people are always quick to believe the worst about others. . .*and are just as eager to pass it on.

Chuck Swindoll, in his book on Nehemiah, warns: "I am personally convinced that the number one enemy of Christian unity is the tongue. It is not drink, not drugs, not poor homes, not inflation, not TV, not even a bad church program—it's the tongue. It is impossible for a leader—or any person for that matter—with a sensitive spirit not to be hurt by a rumor. . .[But] let me say something to those who gossip. If your tongue is a loose tongue, *God is going to have to deal with it.* [1]

That's the tool Sanballat uses here. And he threatens to take the information to Artaxerxes the king. Sliced anyway you want. . .that is blackmail. And it is tactic number two.

There is a third tactic employed by those who try to intimidate. After intrigue and innuendo, *intimidation that sounds spiritual* is used.

And when I entered the house of Shemaiah the son of Delaiah, son of Mehetabel, who was confined at home, he said, "Let us meet together in the house of God, within the temple, and let us close the doors of the temple, for they are coming to kill you, and they are coming to kill you at night." But I said, "Should a man like me flee? And could one such as I go into the temple to save his life? I will not go in." Then I perceived that surely God had not sent him, but he uttered his prophecy against me because Tobiah and Sanballat had hired him. He was hired for this reason, that I might become frightened and act accordingly and sin, so that they might have an evil report in order that they could reproach me (6:10-13).

Shemaiah was one of the Jewish priests. But not only that, he was very friendly with Sanballat and Tobiah. In fact, he was in Sanballat's hip pocket. . .on his payroll. . .in his corner. And here he is pretending to be Nehemiah's friend. And so Shemaiah tells Nehemiah, as if he had received the word from God, that Nehemiah's enemies were his enemies and that they planned to assassinate Nehemiah. But they could both be safe if they hid in the temple.

However, when Shemaiah said, "Let's meet in the house of God, inside the temple," he used a term which refers to the Holy Place in the temple—a place where only the priests were permitted to enter. If he could get Nehemiah in there, it would put Nehemiah in a compromising position destroying his spiritual example. If Nehemiah yields to this "friendly" suggestion, his enemies will expose his fear and use his cowardice to undermine his influence. Furthermore, they will also denounce his faith by pointing to his flagrant disregard of the Old Testament laws.

But the real subtle part to this tactic is that Shemaiah speaks as if his information has come in the form of a prophetic insight. He does not suggest that he is passing on a rumor. No, his words come from God. Isn't it sad how people attempt to drag God into their evil schemes, their gossip, their outright lies? They behave super spiritually, but the whole time—they're out to nail you. They seem concerned about your welfare, as your friend, and always behind the veneer of godliness. The comments are preceded with statements like, "Well, you know I needed to say this because the Lord led me to. . . ." Or, "When I was praying this morning at 2:00 a.m., God spoke to me about this. . . ." Or, "I really believe this is God's will for me to bring this to your attention."

And the entire time the goal is to make mincemeat out of you.

So what are you going to do when people attack you with these kinds of tactics? How do you resist? Let me suggest four techniques of resistance.

The first technique is to *be committed to priorities.*

Nehemiah correctly discerns the insincerity of his enemies and their evil plans. He is not taken in by their overture of reconciliation. . .because he knew their track record. There is no hint anywhere else in the book of Nehemiah that these men wanted to be friends. Nehemiah knew that and so his reply is simple and terse. He tells them he's not moving. "Should a man like me flee?. . .I will not go in!" (6:11).

With Nehemiah it is a matter of principle. The work on the walls was God's appointment for him at this time, and to leave it even temporarily to pursue something else would be to forsake his first priority. He refused to be distracted with lesser matters that would dissipate his energies.

What are your priorities? What keeps you focused and

unmoved when others attempt to intimidate you? What great work are you involved in? Maybe it's a priority to purity. . .to values. . .to integrity and honesty. All of us have a great work to do. God calls us to be Christ-like—in every thought, word, and action. Our priorities in life aren't just marginal options. They are life-determining. Our personality is molded inescapably into the image of what we give priority. We become like what is most important in our life.

We need to be committed to our priorities, confident that they are formed on the solid foundation of God's expectations of obedience and submission in our lives. That is the first technique in resisting intimidation.

The second is distinctly different, but most effective and is what we might term *the ability to rebuke* someone who is distorting the truth.

When Nehemiah finally received the open letter, he wastes no time in sending back his answer. Nor does his answer mince words. He calls the report a lie. "You are just making it up out of your head" (6:8)

Dr. Joseph Parker says this of Nehemiah's response:

"Nehemiah's answer was an answer that might have been shot from a [rifle]. Never attempt to make graceful, apologetic, explanatory statements to your controversial and spiritual enemy. Short answers—cannonball replies— and the enemy will reel. . . . A long and elaborate argument is a long and elaborate opportunity for the devil to take advantage of. . . ."[2]

Tragically, most of the gossip and slander in the Christian community is inaccurate, ungodly, and usually vindictive. All too frequently, it arises from pride and contempt for others and is based on prejudice and misunderstanding.

Do you know what the Apostle Paul says about those who pander in rumor or slander? In I Corinthians 5:11 he lists slander as an offence worthy of church discipline. But in I Corinthians 6:9-10 Paul says that if a person consistently deals in slander, that person is not part of God's kingdom. Slander is serious stuff.

There is a third technique of resistance and that is when we cultivate the fine art of *discernment.*

Then I perceived that surely God had not sent him, but he uttered his prophecy against me because Tobiah and Sanballat had hired him (6:12).

Nehemiah indignantly rejected the scheme of Shemaiah. His words echo across the centuries to us and shout his courage to us. Like Nehemiah, we live in days when we must let our courage be seen by the way we act and speak. It will help us to realize that true courage does not consist in the absence of fear, but in doing what God wants us to do even when we are afraid, disturbed, and hurt. That is what Nehemiah does. But his courage had a foundation, it had an accurate base from which he could act—the Word of God.

Nehemiah's response shows his knowledge of the Word and the extent to which his integrity keeps him from making light of it. He knows that God is the author of truth and that truth is the essence of God's character. God cannot contradict Himself. Shemaiah's proposal was not in harmony with the plain teaching of God's Word, so the prophet was wrong!

For Nehemiah, the issue was clear and simple. The Word of God had spoken and for him to violate the sanctity of the temple would be to disobey the Scriptures and that would be sin. . .so he wouldn't do it.

We lose our character, our integrity, and our ability to discern the issues which confront us when we neglect the personal study of the Scriptures. He could only obey God's commands because he knew God's Word. He was important, busy, and under stress—but none of that kept him from knowing, with a heart-deep knowledge, the Word of Jehovah. When we neglect that kind of knowledge, we find it easy to sacrifice our high ideals of righteousness and integrity on the altars of expediency and selfishness.

Our attitude toward Scripture is desperately important. The choice of that attitude is one of the most difficult and important questions that we decide in all of life. We either choose to believe that the Bible is the infallible Word of God, which means it is entirely trustworthy and reliable, and is to be obeyed, or we decide to reject it. We cannot pick and choose only the part of it that we want to believe.

When people attempt to intimidate you, to frighten you into actions of cowardice that violate your integrity or into actions that involve sinful behavior, be discerning. *Know what God says* and resist them.

That is difficult to do. That's why the final technique is necessary and that is a *total dependence upon God for the necessary strength.*

The question undoubtedly running through Nehemiah's mind is, "What if Artaxerxes believes these charges? What if his mind is poisoned by the lying tongues of my enemies? After all, if he hears it enough times, he may begin to doubt me." Outwardly Nehemiah is unwavering. But inwardly he understood the seriousness of the situation and that is why he depended so much on God.

"Remember, O my God, Tobiah and Sanballat according to these works of theirs, and also Noadiah the prophetess and the rest of the prophets who were trying to frighten me" (6:14).

The encounters with these people have left him shaken. Acutely aware of the strength and smoothness of the enemy and of his own human weakness and vulnerability, Nehemiah rested his case with God.

Nehemiah understood that an open, plain denial and prayer were his only resources. And he held his ground; without a friend. . .he stood alone.

And look what happened. In less than two months, the walls that had been neglected for nearly a century and a half were rebuilt because the people were galvanized into action by the catalyst of Nehemiah's leadership. But notice that with the completion of the walls, the credit is given to God. And the people from the pagan nations surrounding Jerusalem suddenly realized that God was with Nehemiah. They became afraid and lost their self-confidence. The fact is, Nehemiah wasn't alone. He did have a Friend. A Friend who listened to him, who wept for him, who felt his pain, who stood by him, and supported him. His Friend was his God. And with no one else but Him, Nehemiah stood tall.

When our oldest son, Jeremy, was just 4 or 5, I recall driving around our city engaged in theological discussions with him. On one occasion I asked him where he'd like to work when he grew up. I inwardly hoped he'd say the church. He thought about it for awhile, then turned and said, "I'd like to work in a stable!"

"A stable?" I said, "Why a stable?"

With the innocence and sincerity that only children possess, he replied, *"So I can be near Jesus."*

Jeremy is Nehemiah's kind of guy. . . .I wonder if we are!

FOOTNOTES
[1]Charles R. Swindoll, *Hand Me Another Brick,* (Thomas Nelson Publishers, Nashville, TN/ New York, NY, 1978), pp. 131,133. Used with permission.
[2]Joseph Parker, *The People's Bible: Discourses Upon Holy Scripture,* (Hazell, Watson & Viney, LD, London, England, 1889), Vol. X, p. 233.

CHAPTER NINE

THE HEART OF RENEWAL
(Nehemiah 8:1-18)

A 1979 survey conducted by the magazine *Christianity Today* revealed that only 26% of the general public and only 43% of evangelicals believed Jesus Christ to be fully God and fully man.

A more recent Gallup poll revealed that between 1963 and 1982, the percentage of Americans who believed the Bible to be trustworthy and without error dropped from 65% to 37%.

And yet, according to George Gallup, interest in religion is growing in America at an unprecendented rate. But Gallup concluded from all his research:

There is no doubt that religion is growing, but we find little difference in ethical behavior between those who go to church and those who don't. We revere the Bible, but we don't read it. [1]

These facts, all too true today, were just as true in Nehemiah's day, nearly 2400 years ago. As we enter the doorway of Nehemiah chapter eight, we need to realize the people of Jerusalem—with their city completely reconstructed—are now well-ordered, well-defended, and well-governed. But there was still something missing. If the Jerusalem of Nehemiah's day was to remain strong and free, more was needed than city and walls and police protection. A spiritual vacuum existed in the lives of the people. And that is why the leaders of Jerusalem begin to reinforce the stone walls of the city with *a foundation of spiritual values for the people*.

True spiritual renewal comes only when individuals turn

from their religious boredom and moral apathy to God, in repentance and faith. Spiritual renewal involves submission to the authority of the Scriptures. The people of Nehemiah's day realized that.

And all the people gathered as one man at the square which was in front of the Water Gate, and they asked Ezra the scribe to bring the book of the law of Moses which the Lord had given to Israel. Then Ezra the priest brought the law before the assembly of men, women, and all who could listen with understanding, on the first day of the seventh month. And he read from it before the square which was in front of the Water Gate from early morning until midday, in the presence of men and women, those who could understand; and all the people were attentive to the book of the law (8:1-3).

The people gather together for the purpose of hearing the Word of God. But don't miss the fact that it is the *people* who ask that the Word of God be read. Why? Because they were spiritually hungry, and they knew that hunger could only be met through the Scriptures.

Abraham Lincoln once noted: *"I believe the Bible is the best gift that God has ever given to man. All the good from the Saviour of the world is communicated to us through this book. I have been driven many times to my knees by the overwhelming conviction that I had nowhere else to go."*

That is how these people were starting to feel. They wanted the first five books of the Bible—Genesis, Exodus, Leviticus, Numbers, and Deuteronomy—read to them. Now that in itself is amazing. But as Nehemiah summarizes the day's activities, notice that this reading lasted for some six hours. Can you imagine such a thing? These people evidently *stood* for almost six hours, attentively listening to the reading and exposition of the Scriptures.

I can just see us if that happened in one of our church services. We'd get through Genesis okay—there's the flood and all that disaster. Then there is the story of Abraham and the sacrifice of Isaac—with the last minute heroic rescue. There is the political intrigue surrounding Joseph. Yes, we'd get through Genesis. Even the first part of Exodus, although producing a few yawns, could be handled—the plagues and all that stuff. But Leviticus and Numbers—lists of names, fruits, animals, and feasts—forget it. We'd be dropping like flies. Some of us would have to set the alarms on our watches for 60 second intervals just to jolt us back to consciousness. Not these folks. They were serious about spiritual renewal. They wanted a refresher course in God's commands and laws.

During the Protestant Reformation, Martin Luther and his colleagues undertook an extensive campaign of biblical instruction through their sermons. There were three public worship services on Sunday: from 5-6 a.m. on the epistles of Paul; from 9-10 a.m. on the Gospels; and in the afternoon there was another sermon continuing the themes of the morning. Then, on Mondays and Tuesdays, there were sermons on doctrine. On Wednesday, from the Gospel of Matthew; Thursdays and Fridays on the New Testament letters of Peter, James and John, and finally, Saturday evening was devoted to a study of the Gospel of John. Then it started all over again the next morning at 5 a.m.[2] Incredible? Yes, but it's the stuff of renewal.

The people of Nehemiah's day had the same desire. They longed for a spiritual renewal, for God to speak to them. And they knew that He would—through His Word. But God will not speak if we do not allow Him to. Letting God speak to us involves some key ingredients. The first is that we must *give attention to His Word.*

The people had risen very early that morning—well before dawn. They got the kids up, bathed them, and made them as presentable as possible. Then they got onto their four-door camels and went off to the city, where they listened hour after hour to the reading of Scripture. Many of them had not heard the Word of God for years; some had probably not heard it at all. It was a spiritual feast from God's Word.

As Christians, we have a tremendous responsibility to the Word of God. We are called to be "doers of the Word" (James 1:22), but we are also called to be hearers. We need to listen to the Word of God as it is read, with our ears *and* our hearts. We need to listen to the Word of God with all our concentration when it is preached. These people were not there to evaluate, to compare, to criticize, or to ignore the Word of God. . . .They were there to listen!

How about us? Why do we go to church? To be seen? To socialize, catch up on the latest? To meet someone? To look spiritual? If God is to speak to us, if He is to renew us. . .we must listen. And we must listen, first of all, with an underlying appreciation that it is *God's Word.*

These people fully understood the Source of the Scriptures and Who gave it authority. They were attentive because they came with that understanding. That is how we should listen. Secondly, we must listen with an overshadowing sense of *God's presence.* It is just as if He is here, speaking to us. And thirdly, we must listen with a *spirit of prayer.* Praying for ourselves as the Word is preached. Praying that God will change us. Praying also for others when the Word is preached. What a gracious thing to do. And praying for the preacher as he preaches. Praying for the work of the Spirit—to do as He wills.

It is doubtful that there has ever been a genuine revival without the Word of God having a large part in it. Oh how believers need to get back to the basics! We must be willing to pay attention to the Word of God. Study it. Memorize it. Meditate upon it. Let it saturate our thinking. When we are truly in love with the Author of the book, we will also love His Word. We won't let a day pass without spending time alone with God, listening to the silent voice of His eloquent Word teach, rebuke, correct, and train us in righteousness (II Timothy 3:16).

God speaks to us through His Word when we give it our attention. But God also speaks as we approach Him and His Word in *respectful worship.* As Nehemiah tells his story and breaks this day of renewal down into separate details, he goes out of his way to remind us of this key ingredient.

As Ezra the priest unrolled the scroll of the law, even before he opened his mouth to read, *the people were on their feet,* signifying their reverence for the Word of God that was to be read. And that is the astonishing thing. The only focus of that day, apart from a wooden platform built to hold fifteen people, was a scroll and what was written on it. There was no choir, no special music, no program—nothing. . .just the Word of God. Yet it brought them to their feet. . .and then they bowed low and worshiped the Lord with their faces to the ground (8:6).

Dr. Kent Hughes, the senior pastor of the College Church in Wheaton, says it so well:

"They rose in spontaneous reverence and obvious respect for the truth. They gave it a royal reception. Their posture declared how their hearts felt about God's Word. This customary Hebrew reverence for God's Word is a beautiful thing and for us who have so many Bibles and the luxury of so many translations from which to choose, and who take the Scriptures for granted—this is an example of how we ought to reverence God's Word." [3]

How often we fail to do that! Treating casually, even flippantly, that which comes from God, some of us spend more energy arguing over which translation is best. *But when is the last time we approached with reverence the reading of God's Word?*

There is more. Ezra leads the people in prayer before he begins reading. He blesses the Lord. Immediately, the people respond by saying, "Amen, Amen." The heart of the meaning of the word "amen" is the idea of certainty, firmness. The people are saying, "Ezra, whatever you read to us, it will be true. . . .It is certain truth, firm truth. If you read words of comfort, we know they are true. If you read words of conviction and judgment, we know they are true. Whatever is read. . .it is true. We are willing to hear it."

And they demonstrated that attitude not just in words, but also in their posture. We catch a glimpse of the desire of their hearts in their actions. They are so conscious of their need that, as Ezra prays, the whole congregation lifts their arms above their heads with their palms turned heavenward. When a Hebrew stood like that, it was his way of saying, *"Lord, I am empty-handed. I have nothing. Everything I have comes from you."* Their use of the word "amen" means "so be it"—so be your Law to us.

There was a deep reverence for their God. A worshipful humility before the Judge of all the earth and the heavens. No cockiness, no arrogance, no attitude that we have no changes to make, just an incredible awareness of their poverty of spirit before their God. So intense was their brokenness and submission to God, that it drove them to their knees and then to their faces.

When is the last time that you came to the place of wanting—with all your heart—for God to speak to *you*? Not your wife, or your husband. Not your kids, or "old what's his name who really needs this." YOU. . .JUST YOU. When were you so awed by God's person and His Word that it drove you to your knees in brokenness? So many of us come to compare this week's sermon with last week's. . .this week's show with the show we saw at the other church last week. But how many of us come with an attitude of respectful worship and poverty of spirit? That is when God speaks.

Thirteen teachers circulated among the people explaining to them the Scriptures which were read. Their sole function was to instruct the people in the Law, making sure that God's Word was perfectly clear to the people. In fact, Nehemiah 8:8 says that they gave the meaning so that the people could understand what was read. That means that they read it carefully and well and then they explained it section by section.

The Scripture that Ezra read was in Hebrew. Most of the people spoke Aramaic. And although the languages were similar, they needed help. So the text of Scripture was translated and explained section by section.

The heart of renewal springs from that faithful practice today from the man in your pulpit. The responsibility of the preacher is to open the Word of God in such a way that it speaks clearly, plainly, accurately, and relevantly.

"Why?" someone asks. The answer lies in the disturbing fact that as we survey the evangelical pulpits of the world today. . .where do we find that same clarion call from the pulpit? Unfortunately, a spirit like Ezra's is rarely heard. Dr. Martin Lloyd Jones, who succeeded G. Campbell Morgan as the senior pastor at Westminster Chapel in London, England concluded: *". . .The decadent periods and eras in the history of the church have always been those periods when preaching has declined. What is it that always heralds the dawn of a reformation or of a revival? It is renewed preaching!* [4]

When the Word of God is preached with intensity, when it is clearly explained and understood and when we approach it with attention and reverence—*God will speak.* And when He does, we *must respond to his Word.* The people in Jerusalem certainly did (verses 9-10).

The reading, interpretation, and application of the Word

struck a responsive chord in their hearts. They wept because never had they heard it explained so effectively and now they could see what they had been doing. Comparing their own conduct to the standards of God's Word, it was quickly apparent to them how far short they had fallen, and they became *conscious of their sin.*

Don't bypass this. Hearing the Law brought such conviction that the men as well as women and children were overcome with emotion and began to weep. The preaching of the Word was not an antiseptic, cerebral exercise; it was surgery on the heart.

Openly and without shame, they wept over their sin. Think of it. . .thousands of people crying before their God. That is the stuff of renewal.

And it was when the people cried that Nehemiah turned their eyes to their God.

Then Nehemiah, who was the governor, and Ezra the priest and scribe, and the Levites who taught the people said to all the people, "This day is holy to the Lord your God; do not mourn or weep." For all the people were weeping when they heard the words of the law. Then he said to them, "Go, eat of the fat, drink of the sweet, and send portions to him who has nothing prepared; for this day is holy to our Lord. Do not be grieved, for the joy of the Lord is your strength" (8:9-10).

Three times in these verses the people are told to rejoice, not to grieve. Christians must weep over their sin, but their tears should turn to joy. How is that possible? Their tears, like ours, were to become tears of joy as they reflected on the character of their God. He was the source of their joy, their strength.

As they reflected on the character of God, the first thing that would come to mind was *His faithfulness.* .

His faithfulness in allowing the Jews to rebuild the city

against all odds was fresh on their minds. As Ezra read to them from the book of Exodus, of Israel being freed from slavery in Egypt and then kept by God through their wilderness wanderings, they remembered God's faithfulness.

But they would remember, perhaps even more so, *God's great forgiveness* as they listened to the story of Abraham and Isaac, in Genesis, and how God provided a substitute sacrifice for Abraham. They would see again God's forgiveness as He rescued their people from the hands of Pharaoh in Exodus. They would once again tremble at the sacrifice of a perfect lamb whose blood on the doorway of their homes kept them safe as the angel of the Lord came to bring judgment and death to Egypt. They certainly would understand God's forgiveness through the system of sacrifices outlined throughout the book of Leviticus. And as they remembered God's wonderful forgiveness of sin, their guilt and conviction turned to joy.

Isn't that great? Isn't that just like our God? I like the way one unknown poet expressed it: *"Isn't it odd*

> *that a being like God*
> *Who sees the facade*
> *still loves the clod*
> *He made out of sod?*
> *Now isn't that odd?"*

But remember, there can be little joy if there is not, first of all, great conviction of sin. Joy is intensified as we respond to God's Word *through obedience.* These people did that in verses 14 through 17.

As the Word was read, the people were reminded from the book of Leviticus that they were to celebrate the Feast of Tabernacles—a remembrance of God's faithfulness—by living for a week in make-shift booths. As they heard that, they realized that had not been done in Jerusalem in a very long time. So, determined not to be hearers of the Word only, the people accepted the challenge to obedience even though it meant considerable inconvenience for them. They gathered branches and put up booths on the roofs of their homes or in their courtyards. No complaints. . .no whining. . .no rationalizing. . .just OBEDIENCE.

So many Christians today want relief without reprimand. We want solutions to our inner restlessness, but we don't want to change our lifestyles. We want to feel the peace of God while living in direct opposition to the stated commands and directives of His Word. In short, we want the freedom to live life outside the protective fence of God's Word—yet we expect the gate to be left open so we can rush back inside and avoid any negative consequences for our actions.[5]

Not here. Not in Jerusalem. Not on the day God spoke through His Word. On this day, the people *listened with attention* to God's Word. . . .They bowed down in brokenness . . .in *reverence* they waited as the Scriptures were explained to them, and then they wept. They pulled down the masks of hypocrisy and wept before their God. Then they looked up. . . and remembered His faithfulness and His forgiveness—and it brought a smile to their faces. Because they were so freshly in love with their God, and so thankful for His joy, His forgiveness, they*obeyed Him,* without question.

The same course is available to us. Are we serious about obeying our Lord? Do we really want the Lord to renew and revive us?

I find tremendous conviction in Max Lucado's words as he talks about what should happen when we hear God in Christ speak:

> *Something happens to a man when he stands within inches of (Jesus Christ) the Lion of Judah. Something happens when he hears the roar, when he touches the golden mane. Something happens when he gets so close he*

can feel the Lion's breath. Maybe we could all use a return visit. Maybe we all need to witness His majesty. [6]

FOOTNOTES:
[1]Charles Colson, *Who Speaks For God?*, (Crossway Books, Westchester, IL, 1985), p. 88.
[2]Roland H. Bainton, *A Life of Martin Luther*, (Hadder and Stoughton, 1951, New American Library, 1957), pp. 348-349.
[3]R. Kent Hughes, *Hearing The Word*, (College Church in Wheaton, IL, 1985), p. 4.
[4]D. Martin Lloyd-Jones, *Preaching and Preachers*, (Hodder andStoughton, 1971; Zondervan Corporation, Grand Rapids, MI, 1972), p. 24.
[5]Adapted from Tim Kimmel, *Little House on the Freeway*, (Multnomah Press, Portland, OR, 1987), p. 70.
[6]Max Lucado, *No Wonder They Call Him The Savior*, (Multnomah Press, Portland, OR, 1986), p. 164. Used with permission.

CHAPTER TEN

NURTURING REVIVAL
(Nehemiah 9:1-38)

In his introduction to *The Philosophy of History,* G.W. Hegel writes:

> *What experience and history teach is this—that people and governments never have learned anything from history, or acted on principles deduced from it.* [1]

In another section he observes: *"The only thing that man learns from the study of history is that men have learned nothing from history."* [2]

How often that is true in our personal lives. Good advice received last week is easily ignored this week. Failures experienced in November are repeated again in April. Lessons learned yesterday are all too often dismissed as unimportant today. Promises. . .commitments to God. . .made one Sunday have a tendency to be forgotten by the next Sunday.

In Nehemiah 8, the spirit of renewal and revival took hold in the hearts of the people as they began to hunger for God's Word. When the Scripture was read and explained to them, it produced conviction in the hearts of those who heard it. As a result, the people repented of their sin and then demonstrated their repentance through obedience. They observed for the first time since the days of Joshua, the celebration of the Feast of Tabernacles.

But the leaders of the people knew how easy it is to forget the spiritual lessons learned yesterday. So only two days after the events recorded in chapter 8, the people are gathered together again in a great assembly. Now, their leaders are anxious to *conserve and nurture the results of the spiritual revival.*

This was to be more than just a one-day spiritual high. Now the Levites and Nehemiah want to see the results become an ongoing act of the will. That harnessing of will to action came as the people properly worshiped God. We can see that even in their *approach* to worship. . .specifically their *attitude* as they come to worship. The Israelites assembled for a public repentance and confession of sin (9:1). The people fasted to demonstrate their humility and commitment to revival. They wore rough, crudely made garments of goat-hair as a sign of mourning and inner repentance, and they put dirt on their heads as a symbol of their sorrow of heart. They were desperately concerned with their personal state of heart. And it wasn't just a show. They also separated themselves from "foreigners"— those who did not worship God. They were concerned about themselves—their own renewal, not someone else's.

A revival of our hearts and love for God does not last long unless we cultivate an attitude of humility and commitment. But there is also an important *action* necessary as we approach our God for renewal.

> *While they stood in their place, they read from the book of the law of the Lord their God for a fourth of the day; and for another fourth they confesssed and worshiped the Lord their God (9:3).*

For three hours the people stood as the Scriptures were read to them, intent on learning more of the mind and will of God. Then for the next three hours they confessed their personal sins and worshiped God.

Richard Halverson, as he spoke to the United States Senate on January 31, 1983, aptly summarized the intent of the people of Nehemiah's day for us.

> *Repentance. Fundamental to clear thinking about yourself, others, the world—and God. Prerequisite to experiencing His forgiveness, enjoying His love. . .knowing Him.*

*To repent is to be self-critical—to admit need, weak-
ness, sin. It means you stop deceiving yourself about
yourself. . . .Face yourself honestly. And face God. You'll
be amazed how quickly He responds in love, grace,
forgiveness. . . .Let Him change you. No man is truly great
who conceals his sin, refusing to acknowledge his need for
divine mercy. As someone has noted, the blood of Jesus
Christ cleanses only sin—not excuses.* [3]

That is how these people approached their God. That was the
attitude reflected in their actions. And it was only as they came
that way that they could truly worship God. Their worship is
recorded in Nehemiah 9:5-37 as a prayer. In fact, it is the longest
recorded prayer in the Bible. It serves as a model for worship
and revival. It is no accident that as the people are led in worship
their prayer begins by focusing on the glory of God.

*"Arise, bless the Lord your God forever and ever! O may
Thy glorious name be blessed and exalted above all
blessing and praise! Thou alone art the Lord. Thou hast
made the heavens, the heaven of heavens with all their
host, the earth and all that is on it, the seas and all that is
in them. Thou dost give life to all of them and the heavenly
host bows down before Thee"* (9:5-6).

God's glory is the summation of His attributes. Grace, truth,
goodness, holiness. . .all that He is. When we are talking about
the glory of God, we are talking about His intrinsic glory. We
can't give it to Him. He is Who He Is. In order to understand
that, we could express verse 5 by saying, *"Bless the Lord, Who
is above all blessing; praise the God Who is beyond all praise;
stretch out your souls toward Him, Who never can be compre-
hended in all the fulness of His grace and glory."*

I believe that good things happen to our hearts, our attitudes,
when we turn our focus toward the glory of God. The more frequently we focus our thoughts heavenward and thank Him for

His character, for His attributes, for His perfection, we adore our God simply for Who He is. . .not simply for what He does. In *The Knowledge of the Holy*, A.W. Tozer said it so well:

> *When viewed from the perspective of eternity, the most critical need of this hour may well be that the church should be brought back from her long Babylonian captivity, and the name of God be glorified in her again as of old.* [4]

So it was in Nehemiah's moment in time. And their worship continues with the affirmation that God alone is the Lord. They list mighty, powerful things God had done (9:6):

> *You alone are the Lord.*
> *You made the heavens, and all their starry host,*
> *the earth and all that is on it,*
> *the seas and all that is in them.*
> *You give life to everything,*
> *and the multitudes of heaven worship you.*

This is an uncompromising acknowledgment of the uniqueness of God—the point being that nothing in heaven or on earth can challenge God's supremacy.

Worship is not a two-way street. It is a one-way arrow to God. No one can promote God or demote Him. What God is, He is within Himself. To believe in Him adds nothing to His perfection, and doubting Him takes nothing away from Him.

Dietrich Bonhoeffer, immediately after Hitler's takeover of Germany, said:

> *In the church we have only one altar, and that is the altar of the Most High, the Only One, the Lord to whom alone is due honor and adoration; the Creator, before whom all creatures must kneel, before whom the most powerful is nothing but dust. We have no [other] altars for the adoration of men. The worship of God, not of man, happens here at the altar of the church. Anyone who wants anything else may stay away; he cannot stay with us in*

God's house. Anyone who requires an altar for himself or who wants to build one for another man mocks God, and God is not mocked. [5]

Revival is nurtured as we focus on the glory of God. But it is nurtured also when we reflect on His grace and guidance in our lives. The Israelites reviewed Israel's history. . .from their remote beginning with Abraham to their captivity in Babylon. And it is recorded for us to remind us about God.

In the Old Testament, God's choices of people were always because of His grace. Verses 7-15 of Nehemiah 9 remind us of that grace. It is seen in the fact that God began to form a nation with Abraham. Why Abraham? Because God found his heart faithful.

He is the ultimate, self-sufficient Creator God. . . and yet He still chose Abraham and promised him a future with hope. That is grace. But God's grace is also seen because God saw His peoples' bondage in Egypt and, in His sovereignty, intervened as their Redeemer. He saw their affliction, their pain, and heard their cry for deliverance. . .then demonstrated His grace in their lives.

But more than that, He demonstrated His guidance in their lives. The people are reminded of how God broke the power of pharaoh, the most powerful ruler of that day. They see again how God graciously guided them in the trackless desert and made ample provision for their physical needs. They remember how God made them a nation at Mount Sinai and then tangibly assured them of His guidance by writing down standards of behavior for them to follow in the form of His commandments.

Revival. . .spiritual renewal. . .only continues in our lives when we stop to remember our history and learn from our past that God, indeed, is gracious to us and guides us—even if, at this present moment, we cannot appreciate or comprehend that guidance. Perhaps we all should write down our own testament and record God's mighty acts, favors, and grace in our lives. Too many of us have memories that are far too short.

Revival is nurtured as we focus on the glory of God. It is nurtured when we reflect on His grace and guidance. Thirdly, revival is sustained as we consider God's *forgiveness and faithfulness.* The people of Nehemiah's day knew exactly what had gone wrong. Their fathers had become arrogant and stubborn, refusing to obey God's commandments. They chose not to remember all the wonders God had done for them.

In spite of God's evident glory in creation; despite His grace and guidance in their nation's history. . .the Israelites chose to snub their noses at God. According to Nehemiah 9:17, they were so upset with what God was putting them through as they wandered in the wilderness that they actually selected a leader to take them back to Egypt. They reasoned that God had obviously made another one of His colossal mistakes, and they now needed to take charge of their own futures. Then they went even further than that by fashioning an idol in the form of a golden calf and calling it their god, their deliverer.

But sandwiched between descriptions of the people's stubbornness, we find the key statement about the character of our God.

But Thou art a God of forgiveness, gracious and compassionate, slow to anger, and abounding in lovingkindness; and Thou didst not forsake them (9:17).

Nehemiah tells us that our God is characterized by forgiveness. He has forgiven the people in the past, and He goes on doing so time after time.

Furthermore, our God is gracious. He is fundamentally disposed by His nature to be kind, giving, and favorable to His people. As if that is not enough, He is described as being *compassionate.* The word has overtones of the warm, tender feeling that a mother has for her baby.

By all standards of natural justice, God should have written these people (and us!) off. But He did not because He is the God of faithfulness and forgiveness. Joseph Parker, a tremendous preacher from the nineteenth century, wrote of God's forgiveness:

You cannot conceive God's notion of pardon. . . . When God forgives, he does not merely pardon, barely pardon—he does not by some great straining effort of his love, just come within reach of the suppliant, and lay upon his heart the blessing which is besought. He pardons with pardons! When he casts our sins away, it is not into a shallow pool, it is into the depths of the sea. . . . When God takes a man's sins away from him, he puts them as far from him as the east is from the west. Can you tell how far the east is from the west? You cannot; it is an immeasurable line. So, when God comes to pardon us, he pardons with pardons, with pardons again and again, wave upon wave. We have, thank God, some notion of forgiveness; but not until you yourself have entered personally into the mystery of this forgiveness, can you understand or have any hint of the depth of the sea into which God has cast the sins of which we have repented. [6]

That is the wonder of the Christian message: that God loves me with a love that is not turned off by my sins, my failures, my inadequacies, my insignificance. I am not a nameless insect waiting to be crushed by an impersonal boot. I am not a miserable offender cowering under the glare of an angry deity. I am a person beloved by God Himself. And that love has reached me, not because I have earned God's favor, not because I have anything to boast about, but because of Who He is. . .the God of forgiveness and faithfulness.

In the desert wanderings, the people lacked nothing and their clothes did not wear out. Despite their rejection of the Lord,

God stood by His people, kept His promises, and met their deepest and most basic needs. He does the same for us—even though there may be a price to pay and consequences to face for our rebellion.

John MacArthur, pastor of Grace Community Church in California, said,

You know how to trust God in the present? Watch Him in the past. God has already established the pattern of his faithfulness. . . .Do you know one good reason to study the Old Testament? To find out that God is a faithful God. And if you can see Him vindicated all through the past history of man's age, you can certainly trust Him in this moment. [7]

Revival grows deeper as we comprehend the forgiveness and faithfulness of our God. but there is something else we must come to grips with if revival is to continue. We must understand our *rebellion against God and His method of rescue.*

God graciously allowed Israel to come into the promised land, but instead of obeying God's commands, they ignored Him and concentrated on their luxuries.

And because they threw God's Word behind their backs, then killed the prophets He sent to them, and committed acts of contempt against Him, they were punished as a nation. Enemies plundered their country and became God's instruments of judgment. Then, when the people repented, God graciously rescued them. For awhile they would live as though God existed in their lives, but given enough rope—they'd hang themselves and disobey again, so God would allow punishment to occur again. And that cycle repeated itself over and over in their lives.

God is the God of grace and forgiveness, but He will not wink at sin in our lives. As Rudyard Kipling said: *"The sin ye do two by two, ye must pay for one by one."* [8]

In *Three Steps Forward Two Steps Back,* Charles Swindoll

noted: *"When we choose to walk away from the Lord and shake our fists at His grace, He sets the hounds of heaven against us. He does not let His children run wayward or play in the streets of the world without exerting a great deal of discipline. God is very serious about that. You never find a place in the Bible where God no longer calls the people of Israel His children— they're still His, and so are you if you have accepted Him as your personal Savior from sin—but that does not mean that you cannot come under His discipline."* [9]

Judgment, or punishment, is not God's way of saying, *"I'm through with you."* It is not a mark of abandonment by God. Rather, it is the last loving act of God to bring us back; it is, in fact, the last resort of love. C.S. Lewis said, *"God whispers to us in our pleasures; He speaks to us in our work; (but) He shouts at us in our pain. It is his megaphone to rouse a deaf world."* [10] Every one of us knows that there have been times when we would not listen to God; we would not pay attention to what His Word says, until one day God hit us over the head with the 2 x 4 of our lives. Then we begin to listen.

That is what God is doing here. Because even in His punishment, His rescuing salvation is evident. The Scriptures record for us how God delivered His people time after time. They were arrogant, rebellious, stubborn—but each time they genuinely repented and turned back to God in obedience, He forgave them. Why?

Nevertheless in Thy great compassion Thou didst not make an end of them or forsake them, for Thou art a gracious and compassionate God (9:31).

That constant theme. . .that continual reminder of grace brought these people to the final element in the steps necessary to keep revival alive. . .a *deep reverence for God* and our *ultimate response.*

In Nehemiah 9:32 we finish the history lesson and are

brought quickly back to the present tense. In essence we have come full circle. . .to where we began in verse 5. The chapter ends where it started. . .with a deep reverence for Who God is. But there is a major difference, now. As they are led in prayerful worship they say, in effect, "We deserved everything we got! We brought it on ourselves by our own actions. God is not to blame. . .we are! And as their history has been reviewed, it brings them to a new spiritual commitment to God. They sign their names, make a binding written agreement between themselves and the Lord (9:38).

For the time, at least, Israel determines to learn from her past and to obey God more perfectly in the future. There is a desire for a new relationship with their God, a renewed relationship. It was so important that they wanted an agreement to hold them to their obedience. . .to their commitment.

And the context indicates that this agreement or promise was entered into voluntarily by the people. The seriousness of it is seen in the fact that they put it in writing and take upon themselves a curse if they don't follow through. Essentially, Nehemiah and his peers prayed: *"Lord, we don't want this to be simply an empty series of words. We want it to be a promise that is nailed down. We declare today our dependence on you. And we're signing our names to prove that we'll keep our promise."*

Revival in the life of an individual and the life of a church begins when we approach our God humbly, confessing our sin. It is nurtured as we worship the glory of God. . .as we reflect on His grace and guidance in our lives. . .and remain constantly aware of His forgiveness and faithfulness. Revival is nurtured when we understand that our disobedience will produce negative consequences as God attempts to bring us back to Him in a posture of reverence. But none of that will have an enduring result unless it brings us to the response of obedience and commitment. . .prompted by His wonderful grace.

FOOTNOTES:

[1]G.W.F. Hegel, *Philosophy of History, Introduction,* cited in *The Oxford Dictionary of Quotations,* Third Edition, (Oxford University Press, Oxford, NY, 1980), pp. 244:8.

[2]Cited by Bergen Evans in *Dictionary of Quotations,* (Bonanza Books, New York, NY, 1968), p. 317.3.

[3]Richard Halverson, *No Greater Power,* (Multnomah Press, Portland, OR, 1986), pp. 145,146,153.

[4]A.W. Tozer, *The Knowledge of the Holy,* (Harper and Row Publishers, New York, NY, 1978), p. 121.

[5]Dietrich Bonhoeffer, "Gideon," in *Twenty Centuries of Great Preaching,* (Word Inc., Dallas, TX, 1971), XII, pp. 127-128.

[6]Joseph Parker, *The People's Bible*, Vol. XXV, Ephesians-Revelation, Hazell, Watson, and Viney, Ltd., Creed Lane, Ludgate Hill, E.C. (London, England, 1895), p. 5.

[7]John MacArthur, Sermon, "How to Glorify God," from Dallas Seminary file, Dallas, TX.

[8]Rudyard Kipling, cited by *Oxford Dictionary of Quotations,* Third Edition, (Oxford University Press, New York, NY, 1980), p. 303:20.

[9]Charles Swindoll, *Three Steps Forward Two Steps Back,* (Thomas Nelson Publishers, Nashville, TN, 1980), pp. 170-171. Used with permission.

[10]C. S. Lewis, *The Problem of Pain*, (Collier Books, Macmillan Publishing, New York, NY, 1962), p. 93.

CHAPTER ELEVEN

COMMITMENT, SACRIFICE— AND YOU
(Nehemiah 10:1-39)

A man said, *"If I had some extra money, I would give it to God. But I have just enough to support myself and my family."* And the same man said, *"If I had some extra time, I would give it to God. But every minute is taken up with my job, my family, my clubs and what have you, every single minute."* And the same man said, *"If I had talent, I would give it to God. But I have no lovely voice; I have no special skill. I've never been able to lead a group; I can't think cleverly or quickly the way I would like to."*

So God gave that man money, time, and glorious talent. And then He waited. He waited and continued to wait. Then after awhile, God took all those things right back from the man—the money, the time, and the glorious talent. After awhile, the man sighed and said, *"If only I had some of that money back, I'd give it to God. If only I had some of that time I'd give it to God. If I could only rediscover some of that glorious talent, I'd give it to God."*

I wonder if there isn't more truth in this imaginary scenario than we'd like to admit.

The famous long distance runner, Jim Ryan, who set the record for a mile when he was 18-years-old, talks about his training, saying, *"I would run until I felt I couldn't take another step, then I would run until I felt my lungs were going to burst. When I came to that state, then I would run until I thought I was going to pass out. When I did this, I was making progress. "*

The same thing is true when we talk about our spiritual lives. If we approach it casually, with only a daydream intensity, we should not be surprised that our commitment, like a merry-go-round, seems to keep us going in circles, rather than forward.

I remember hearing a professor say, *"Cults are the promissory notes that the church never paid. "* His point was that if the church were what it should be, the cults would never get off the ground. Today's church calls its people to so little. Meanwhile, young people are looking for something to give their lives to wholeheartedly. So, when a cult leader comes along demanding total commitment, they are challenged. The vision is big enough to command their attention.

In our dust-raising journey with Nehemiah, we have begun to feel the pulse of spiritual renewal. We have felt the hot breath of revival raising the hair on our necks. And we have come to understand that it begins with an unquenchable thirst for the Word of God. Then, as with the people of Nehemiah's era, the renewal continues as we become more aware of who our God is. As we review our own personal histories—and recall our past failures and sins—we are struck with the majesty of God's faithfulness and forgiveness in our lives. When that happens, we are catapulted into a lifestyle of obedience.

In a nutshell, that is precisely what has happened to the people surrounding Nehemiah, over 2,400 years ago. It prepared them for the signing of a written document. . .a promise of commitment between them and their God. As their leaders led them in worship and the study of the Scriptures for the first time in a long time, they felt as if their backs were to the wall . . .that it was time to leave their faith or to commit to it. They sensed that perhaps they had been committed only to the short haul, not the long-distance marathon, and now a choice had to be made. They knew, in their heart of hearts, that they must now step off the merry-go-round and take their commitment to God seriously.

And so they did. Before we consider the specifics of the document they signed though, let's look at the **kinds of people involved** in this.

I'd suggest, first of all, that the people involved are *unknowns*. In 84 individual names we see Nehemiah, the governor, listed first and then 83 other names follow. I haven't got a clue who those people are. . .except that they were involved in some form of leadership in Jerusalem. In verse 28, the *"rest of the people"* involved in this commitment are not even listed by name, only by function or job description.

It's just a list. A list of names, a list of strange names at that. But for Nehemiah it's not just a list. It is a roll call of remembrances. These are people of whom Nehemiah is proud and thankful for. . .because they put their spiritual lives on the line. They joined him in a spiritual commitment of immense proportion.

The point: You don't have to have a big name to be committed. You don't have to be easily recognized by others. You don't need money or extraordinary talent. You don't have to be recognized or known at all to be committed. In fact, sometimes it helps if you're not.

Oswald Chambers, in his book *Man's Weakness—God's Strength,* said,

> *God can achieve His purpose either through the absence of human power and resources, or the abandonment of reliance on them. All through history God has chosen and used nobodies, because their unusual dependence on Him made possible the unique display of His power and grace. He chose and used somebodies only when they renounced dependence on their natural abilities and resources.* [1]

Do you have a piece of paper? Write down these words: *"I am thankful to God for these spiritually committed people."* And then write a name. You choose the name. You remember the name. Write another name, and another. Keep that list, because to you it's not a list. . .it's a remembrance.

The people involved were ordinary folks. But there's something else about them. Entire families made this commitment. They gave their support to the ones who were the legal signors and, in doing so, accepted the terms. But they did it as a family. And when you think about it, that would include the age group we would call *"twenty and under."* Young people stood with their parents, parents stood with their kids, husbands with wives, wives with husbands—committed spiritually as a family.

To what is your family committed? The widely acclaimed 17-year study published in the book, *Inside the Criminal Mind,* concluded in 1984 that crime is not the result of environment or poverty, but of wrong moral choices. Harvard professors James Wilson and Richard Herrnstein concluded in 1985 that such moral choices are determined by moral conscience, which is shaped early in life and *most profoundly by the family.* Without the lessons the family alone can teach—commitment to God and duty to fellow man become alien concepts.[2]

That's why here, as soon as their children were old enough to catch on, their parents involved them in spiritual commitment.

Who are the people involved here? Ordinary unknowns. Families, including kindergartners, elementary-aged children, and adolescents. They didn't care what anybody else did or thought. They stepped off the merry-go-round. And that helps us see the third element of who were involved—*the rest of the people joined with their families and their leaders* (10:29).

We can't get away from this revival without the impression

that everyone is in it together. *Everyone* who could understand shared in this promise of commitment. This isn't just another boring Old Testament list. This is a statement of *unity.*

The rest of the people voluntarily came forward to declare their spiritual commitment. Although they did not sign the document, they bound themselves by an oath to obey the conditions. . .regardless of the cost. Without realizing it, they anticipated the call that Jesus Christ gave 450 years later.

Jesus said then—and today—*"If anyone wishes to after Me let him deny himself, and take up his cross, and follow Me"* (Matthew 16:24). No threats. No intimidation. No manipulation or coercion through fear. Just, "If you will, then get busy, get serious, and come!"

But in going, we must agree to the terms. We must understand *the purpose of our commitment.* These people certainly did. They carved it into the cement sidewalk of their lives. They programmed it into the computer disks of their day-to-day experiences. They wove it into the fabric of their souls.

. . .*All those who had knowledge and understanding, are joining with their kinsmen, their nobles, and are taking on themselves a curse and an oath to walk in God's law, which was given through Moses, God's servant, and to keep and to observe all the commandments of God our Lord and His ordinances and His statutes (10:28c-29).*

This is a determination, a resolution to be faithful. And so serious were they that the promise was reinforced by a curse—meaning they were calling disaster down upon themselves if they should go back on their word.

These people made a corporate decision to submit themselves obediently to the authority of Scripture. They know that they cannot expect God's blessing without being obedient to His Word. They also know that they have to act responsibly before Him. To pray for His blessing and then to go their own way will not work. So, their purpose is to obey the Word of God.

Every time I read these words of A.W. Tozer, I feel the heat of conviction turned up around me.

Truth divorced from life is not truth in its Biblical sense, but something else and something less....No man is better for knowing that God in the beginning created the heaven and the earth. The devil knows that, and so did Ahab and Judas Iscariot. No man is better for knowing that God so loved the world of men that He gave His only begotten Son to die for their redemption. In hell there are millions who know that. Theological truth is useless until it is obeyed. [3]

Do you still have a piece of paper? Turn it over and we'll make another list. Actually, it will be two lists. On one side write down the traits that God has grafted into your life over the last three years and the areas of obedience you have consciously responded to in that time. Now, on the other side—you don't have to show this to anyone—write down three areas of disobedience in your life right now. It might relate to the use of your tongue...it could be anger...maybe jealousy. You know what it is. Write it down. Now today, get alone for a moment and make a promise to God that you will consciously submit in obedience to Him in those three areas.

William Barclay, a New Testament scholar, put it this way:

It is possible to be a follower of Jesus without being a disciple; to be a camp-follower without being a soldier of the king; to be a hanger-on in some great work without pulling one's weight. Once someone was talking to a great scholar about a younger man. He said, "So and so tells me that he was one of your students." The teacher answered devastatingly, "He may have attended my lectures, but he was not one of my students." There is a world of difference between attending lectures and being a student. It is one of the supreme handicaps of the Church that in the Church there are so many distant followers of Jesus and so few real disciples. [4]

Do you still have the lists? The ones about obedience and disobedience? Compare your list to the list these people prepared. They were not satisfied with simply stating the purpose of their promise generically. They wanted to be specific. . .to have a clear target. So they commit themselves to certain details.

The first detail is *separation.*

The Israelites determine right off the top to no longer intermarry with *"the peoples of the land"* (10:30). That phrase refers to those who worship other gods. . .who do not have the same faith as the Hebrews. The religious practices of the people around them were particularly immoral and incredibly detrimental to the moral life of the nation.

Derek Kidner, in his excellent commentary on Nehemiah, wrote:

> *The Old Testament law consistently condemned marriage to non-believers. But the pull to climb socially was very tempting in those days, and marriage to an unbeliever offered an attractive ladder. . . .And lest the Christian should think it is no longer a live issue, [the apostle] Paul expounds the [same principle] with unanswerable logic and passionate intensity in II Corinthians 6:14 when he writes: "Do not be unequally yoked together with unbelievers."* [5]

Nothing alters our lives like marriage. For two people who love the Lord, their relationship holds unlimited potential for personal growth and development. But without this basic spiritual unity, the marriage lacks the one element that can give it strength, stability, and maximum fulfillment. A believer cannot rationalize entering into such a relationship with a non-Christian under the pretense of winning his mate to Christ. The success rate in that area is dismal—to say the least.

Stripped of its pious language and weak-kneed pseudo-faith, the prayer of a Christian about to marry an unbeliever really says something like this:

"Dear Father, I don't want to disobey You, but I must have my own way at all costs. For I love what You do not love, and I want what You do not want. So please be a good God and deny Yourself, and move off Your throne, and let me take over. If You don't like this, then all I ask is that You bite Your tongue and say or do nothing that will spoil my plans, but let me enjoy myself." [6]

The people of Nehemiah's day knew that—at last! They now acknowledged that by marrying those who do not hold sacred the things which they regarded as being holy, there would be a breakdown in their homes. But more than that, that breakdown in the home would have an impact on their society at large. When spiritual realities are set aside, moral values deteriorate.

That is why, in part, they determined to operate their corporate lives differently on their day of worship. They changed the way they did business in order to honor the Lord.

As for the peoples of the land who bring wares or any grain on the sabbath day to sell, we will not buy from them on the sabbath or a holy day; and we will forego the crops the seventh year and the exaction of every debt (10:31).

By this practice, they reminded themselves of their unique calling as a special people of God, and they set themselves distinctly apart from those who did not worship God. This was not a meaningless promise, either. They desired distinctiveness. They understood that when spiritual realities are set aside, values slide.

For us, this is nowhere else more clearly seen than in our network television fare. . .and the obvious effects in American society. In 1989, the research team of Lichter and Rothman made the most in-depth study ever conducted of those who are responsible for our entertainment programs. Those researched represented the "cream of television's creative community."

Of the people who control television, who tell us what we will watch, 59% were raised in Jewish homes, 25% in Protestant homes, and 12% in Catholic homes. At the present time 93% of these people say they seldom or never attend worship and 44% currently claim no religion at all.

Lichter and Rothman found that 97% of these people believe a woman has the right to decide on abortion, only 5% strongly agree that homosexuality is morally wrong; only 16% agree that adultery is morally wrong, 69% feel the government should redistribute the income in our society, and 45% believe the government should guarantee everyone a job.

When asked what groups they would give the most influence to if they could reshape society, they place religion next to last, listed only above the military.

Quoting the study, ". . .*Two out of three believe that TV entertainment should be a major force for social reform. This is perhaps the single most striking finding in our study. According to television's creators, they are not in it just for the money. They also seek to move their audience toward their own vision of the good society.*" [7]

We live in a very strange time in which I think it could be truthfully said that common decency is no longer common.

For instance, the 14-year-old boy in Mississippi who speculated: *"What would it be like to kill someone?"*

He took a younger friend out among some trees, beat him to death over a sustained time with a baseball bat, left the body, went and joined in a snowball fight, then boasted to a friend that he'd just killed a friend. Asked him if he wanted to see the body.

Finally, through an anonymous tip, the police discovered the body and the murder. The psychiatrist who examined that 14-

year-old boy, said: *"Internally he does not know the difference between right and wrong. He knows the theory, but he doesn't know how to put it into action."*

Or the incident in Kissimmee, Florida: A 9-year-old child took a 3-year-old, tossed him into the deep end of a pool, and watched him with fascination while he drowned.

And we wonder: *"What has happened?"*

Or did you notice the newspaper headline that reported: *"Ethics class avoids teaching right and wrong"?* [8]

The people of Nehemiah's day made a commitment to separation. They said, *"Hey, we won't shrug our shoulders, yawn and say, 'It doesn't matter,' when our kids want to mix and mingle with the crowd. It does matter. . .our values matter, and we will find them in the Scripture."*

The first detail of obedience is separation. The second is what we can call *sensitivity.*

. . .And we will forego the crops the seventh year and the exaction of every debt (10:31).

The laws of the Old Testament sought to prevent the abuse of people. For example, interest bearing loans were forbidden between the Jews. In fact, after a seven-year period, any outstanding loans were to be forgiven, because generosity was commanded as the rule. Sensitivity to needs was encouraged. The people were also to leave their fields uncultivated during that seventh year. This reminded them that God was the Provider and Owner of their resources. They were simply tenants.

That had to be tough! Think of the lost revenue. Think of the loss in sales production. . .the quotas not met. Good night. . . that's crazy! Until we stop to remember that these people were coming out of captivity. They have already been devastated by famine and loan sharks just in their short time back in Jerusalem. They needed time and generosity to bounce back, to get their feet on the ground. And so the people. . .sensitive to their needs. . .made a commitment to obey God's law even in these areas. They stayed sensitive to mercy.

How? Because mercy is seeing someone without food and giving him food. Mercy is seeing a person begging for love and giving that love. Mercy is seeing someone lonely and giving them company. *Mercy is meeting the need, not just feeling it.*

Do you still have your list of remembrances? The first one with the names? Are there some names of spiritually committed people on it? Now write beside each name three needs those people might have right now. Do you know what they are? Even spiritually committed people have needs. Are you sensitive to those needs. . .will you attempt to meet them? That is the second detail these people committed their lives to meeting.

There is a third and final one. We can call it a *commitment to sacrifice* for the Lord's work. Nehemiah articulates that in verses 32, 33, and 39:

We also placed ourselves under obligation to contribute yearly one third of a shekel for the service of the house of our God: for the showbread, for the continual grain offering, for the continual burnt offering, the sabbaths, the new moon, for the appointed times, for the holy things and for the sin offerings to make atonement for Israel, and all the work of the house of our God. . . . For the sons of Israel and the sons of Levi shall bring the contubution of the grain, the new wine and the oil, to the chambers; there are the utensils of the sanctuary, the priests who are ministering, the gatekeepers, and the singers. Thus we will not neglect the house of our God.

The people pledged themselves to maintain their place of worship and those who served in it. This decision required a commitment that was open-ended and which made its mark upon the everyday life of these people.

As we read the details of their promise in these verses, we discover that not only will they insure that the required sacrifices are provided, but they will even make certain there is an adequate supply of wood for the altar. Furthermore, the extent of the Lord's claim on their lives will touch all they have—their children, cattle, produce, even the wine and oil. They realized that it is not only the best that belongs to God, but also the first. It would have been presumptuous for them to enjoy something before first of all giving God His portion.

It is significant to see that by signing or agreeing with this promise, the people have surrendered their pocketbooks. Apparently, the revival had struck deep. They determine, once and for all not to neglect the house of God.

That's remarkable. Because the temptation for them—in a day of economic recession and great personal needs—was to begrudge the effort and expense associated with the temple. They had enough problems. . .they didn't need to add this to them. But these people refused to fall for that kind of ungodly thinking. They committed themselves to financial sacrifice. Personal stewardship continues to be an incredibly reliable and accurate index of commitment to the Lord and His work.

Okay, do you still have your list? The second one. . .the one that listed areas of disobedience? Does your giving pattern need to be on it? Some researchers estimate that evangelical Christians give an average of 2 percent of their income.[9] Would the word sacrifice describe your giving patterns? Has renewal hit you that deeply? According to *USA Today,* 60% of those who make religious donations give less than $100 a year or $1.90 per week.[10]

Sacrifice. I think of a magnificent story of 400 A.D. An Asian monk by the name of Telamaucus was sitting in his lonely cell meditating. He felt that God was saying, "Telamaucus, go to Rome."

He thought to himself, "What do I want to do in Rome? But if God wants me there, I will go." So he took all his possessions, put them in his little bag, threw it over his shoulder, and started down the long road west to Rome. When he got there, the streets were filled with hustle and bustle and confusion and excitement. He asked someone, "What is going on?"

The person said, "Oh, this is *the* day in the Coliseum. Today we have gladiators. Animals killing animals. Animals killing men. Men killing animals. And men killing men for the glory of Caesar."

The monk said, "Maybe that is what God wants me here for." He took his seat way down front in the amphitheater, which held 80,000 people. The athletes came out and the gladiators came out and the animals were let out. After the gladiators passed by saying, "Hail to Caesar," the fighting and the bloodshed began. The monk did the only thing he could. He jumped over the barrier, out onto the field, and he called out, "In the name of Christ, forbear." They laughed. Laughter rippled through the crowd of 80,000. The gladiators came rushing at one another, almost ignoring the monk, and sent him spinning off. Then the crowd began to shout, "Run him through. Run him through." But he stood up again and said, "In the name of Christ, forbear."

One of the gladiators took the flat of his sword and slapped him into the dust. But as he lay in the dust he yelled, "In the name of Christ, forbear." A second gladiator went over, took his sword, and ran it through Telamaucus's stomach, and the blood began to color the sand. Cheers went up from the stadium as his last words whispered, "In the name of Christ, forbear." But in the upper tier, one man stood and walked out. Seconds later, four or five others stood and walked out. Within minutes the place was empty, and it was the last known gladiatorial contest in the history of Rome.

Sacrifice.

FOOTNOTES:

[1] Oswald Chambers, "Man's Weakness - God's Strength," *Missionary Crusader*, (December 1964), p. 7.

[2] Cited by Charles Colson, *Kingdoms in Conflict,* (William Morrow & Co., Inc., New York, N.Y. and Zondervan Publishing House, Grand Rapids, MI, 1987), pp. 90-91.

[3] Taken from *Of God and Men* by A. W. Tozer. Copyright 1970, Christian Publications, 3825 Hartzdale Dr., Camp Hill, PA 17011. Used by permission.

[4] William Barclay, *The Gospel of Luke, The Daily Study Bible,* (The Saint Andrew Press, Edinburgh, Scotland, 1964), p. 203.

[5] Derek Kidner, *Ezra & Nehemiah,* (InterVarsity Press, Downers Grove, IL, 1979), p. 115.

[6] Ray C. Stedman, *Life by the Son: Expository Studies in I John,* (Word, Inc., Dallas, TX, 1980), p. 361.

[7] From an editorial in the *National Federation for Decency's Journal,* March 1986, p. 2, by Don Wildmon, Executive Director.

[8] Ben Haden, "Bonding Crisis," *Changed Lives*, (Ben Haden Evangelical Association, Inc., 1988), pp. 10-11.

[9] Gene A. Getz, *A Biblical Theology of Material Possessions,* (Moody Press, Chicago, IL, 1990).

[10] *USA Today*, April 24, 1990.

CHAPTER TWELVE

KEEPING US HONEST
(Nehemiah 13:1-31)

In the court of King Charles I, the most remarkable knight of all was Sir Jeffery Hudson. Immortalized in the art and literature of the 17th century, Sir Jeffery was no mere legend. His deeds of valor, his life of romance and adventure are a matter of record.

From an early age, Jeffery Hudson was destined to royal favor. At age 9 he was taken into the service of the Duke and Duchess of Buckingham. There he was trained, later to be presented to the King and Queen of England. When he was 11-years-old, he was accepted into the British diplomatic service. His first mission involved a trip to France; the return voyage, of which, was interrupted by pirates off the coast of Dunkirk. The gallantry he demonstrated throughout the attack would typify him in later years; a life of adventure was just beginning.

Still in his teens, he sailed in Holland with the earls of Warwick and Northampton to aid the Dutch in their war of independence against the Spaniards. By 1637, reports of Jeffery's courage reached England, and a year later, at the age of 19, Jeffery was greeted in his homeland as a hero. He was knighted Sir Jeffery Hudson. The ladies of the royal court fought for his attention. A book was written about him.

Becoming a captain in the King's army, Sir Jeffery fought bravely against the Puritans who sought to overthrow Charles I. When the royal cause was lost, he escaped with the Queen to France. From that time until the day he died, he experienced an incredible succession of exploits, duels to the death, unjust imprisonment and escape, world travel, battles with pirates, and slavery among the Turks.

At 39 he returned to England and the friendly court of Charles II. For seven years he maintained his reputation as a gallant knight before retiring to the quiet life of a country squire. But retirement was too quiet for this courageous adventurer. So, in 1679, at the age of 60, he emerged from the comfort of his country home and pension to join the secret service of the King.

Of all his perils, however, there was one adventure in particular from which Sir Jeffery narrowly escaped with his life. While he had easily survived the fields of battle and the fields of honor, one day—in a very embarrassing manner—Sir Jeffery nearly drowned in the washbasin!

How could that be? The reason is found in the picture remnants that survive him. Portraits of Sir Jeffery and the Queen hang today in Hampton Court. And his clothing has been preserved in the Ashmolean Museum in Oxford.

For the courageous Sir Jeffery Hudson, the knight whose days were laced with heroism and intrigue, the remarkable soldier, the valiant warrior, Sir Jeffery Hudson, in his stocking feet. . .WAS ONLY 18 INCHES TALL![1]

I have no idea how tall Nehemiah was. I don't even know how old he was, but regardless of his physical stature or age he, like Sir Jeffery Hudson, stands tall in the annals of history as a man of courage and conviction. Our world looks today for such men and women.

Alexander Solzhenitsyn is an astute observer of history and our time. He understands them better than most. It is because of that that his words haunt me when he writes: "Must one point out that from ancient times a decline in courage has been considered the beginning of the end."[2]

One of the primary messages I want my sons to receive, one

of the prayers I long for them to say is not, "God, keep Dad safe today," but rather, "God, make my dad brave, and if there are hard things that he must do, give him the strength to do them."

Nehemiah. . .if he has taught us anything. . .has taught us the crucial importance of courage. . .of the strength of character that allows us to do the hard things because they are the right things. That was true at the beginning of his story, and it is true as his story draws to a close. . .as the light of history fades from his life. It is the story we find in Nehemiah 13.

As the sun sets on Nehemiah's assignment and we follow his taillights, as it were, into this chapter, bear in mind that there is a gap of time between the events of chapter 12 and those of chapter 13. The first 12 chapters of Nehemiah cover approximately seven months of time. Between chapters 12 and 13, the balance of Nehemiah's term as governor, there are $11^1/2$ years, plus an additional period of time when Nehemiah returned to his position in Persia working for King Artaxerxes (13:6).

During his absence from Jerusalem, the opposition party—made up of the high priest, his family, and the influential people of the city—reverse the direction of reform that Nehemiah had so courageously established. In fact, while Nehemiah was away, permissiveness replaced renewal and revival. What was once regarded as wrong is now openly practiced without shame.

It is most likely that Nehemiah once again heard disturbing reports from Jerusalem as he served King Artaxerxes. . .and once again, asked for and received a second leave of absence. Upon his return to Jerusalem, he finds that the reformation movement that began so well is no longer going anywhere. The solemn promises of the past have been tossed out the window of the people's lives.

Isn't it interesting that all the trouble developed when Nehemiah exited stage right. Once he was out of sight, people did what they knew was wrong. The old, human nature was at work then, just as now. As employees. . .what kind of work do we produce when our supervisor is absent? As husbands. . .at the office or when we travel, what is our behavior like? As Christians. . .when we are with non-Christians, how do we behave?

It is into that kind of environment that Nehemiah returns to deal with *the problems that surfaced* in his absence. And when he got back to Jerusalem, he wasn't smiling. One Old Testament scholar observes:

If, on his first visit, (Nehemiah) had been a whirlwind, on his second he was all fire and earthquake to a city that had settled down in his absence to a comfortable compromise with the Gentile world. [3]

The first problem that flamed Nehemiah's fire was a misuse of God's house.

During Nehemiah's absence Tobiah used his influence with Eliashib to gain an entrance into the temple. We're told the two were "closely associated" (13:4). That either means that they were related by marriage, or that they were just "tight" politically. At any rate, Tobiah was able to pressure the high priest into surrendering the proper use of some of the temple facilities and, instead, providing him with a penthouse suite. The high priest knew better. The temple area was given over to worship . . .not comfortable real estate dealings.

Chuck Swindoll, in analyzing this problem, hits the nail on the head.

Tobiah. . .had been an enemy of God and a thorn in Nehemiah's side. Nehemiah had faced him repeatedly as Tobiah had tried to stop construction of the wall and had personally criticized, attacked and assaulted Nehemiah. But all the way through the Jerusalem project, Nehemiah made sure Tobiah never got inside the walls. Tobiah is the classic example of the rebellious unbeliever or the carnal Christian who tries every way in the world to thwart the work of God. However, while Nehemiah was away Eliashib. . .says, "Let's clear out the area normally given to this storage and provide a nice place for Tobiah." [4]

Sometimes friendship supersedes right. Loyalties of long standing. . .friendships that count the years. . .tend to blur our vision of priorities that are right. Often we don't even see it. Or, if we do, we want to define it as a reasonable compromise. It usually isn't, especially when it involves lowering God's standards. That is what has happened here.

But there is a second problem that Nehemiah stumbled over upon his return.

The people were no longer giving to the support of the Temple, which included, in addition to money, food for the Levites, the religious leaders (13:10). Maybe they figured they could invest their money more profitably elsewhere. Maybe they were reacting to the misuse of the temple. But since Nehemiah's departure, a grudging attitude marked the day. Now the tendency was to give as little as possible. As a result, the Levites were going hungry. Sadly, the portions dedicated to them had not been given. In order to escape starvation, these men had moved out into the country and gone back to farming to support their families.

Instead of spending time leading the people in spiritual matters, they were working just to stay alive. The bottom line had become finances and the work of God was suffering.

In those days I saw in Judah some who were treading wine presses on the sabbath, and bringing in sacks of grain and loading them on donkeys, as well as wine, grapes, figs, and all kinds of loads, and they brought them into Jerusalem on the sabbath day. So I admonished them on the day they sold food. Also men of Tyre were living there who im-

ported fish and all kinds of merchandise, and sold them to the sons of Judah on the sabbath, even in Jerusalem. Then I reprimanded the nobles of Judah and said to them, "What is this evil thing you are doing, by profaning the sabbath day? Did not your fathers do the same so that our God brought on us, and on this city, all this trouble? Yet you are adding to the wrath on Israel by profaning the sabbath" (13:15-18).

Robert Foster paraphrases for us what is happening here: *Profit at any price businessmen had turned the Sabbath Day into a terrific dollar asset. The "day of rest" had become big bucks for them. The Holy Day was a short-cut to the 1st Citizens Bank of Jerusalem."* [5]

Funny how that happens, isn't it? We constantly need to check and recheck what money is doing to us—have a periodic money check-up. All of us need to learn to say "no" to money because, if we don't face up to the damage it causes, we may find ourselves and the institutions we love destroyed by it...just like in Jerusalem.

Phillip Yancey graphically portrays the battle we face:

In its effect on me, money works much like the temptations of lust and pride. I holds me in a pythonic grip. It attracts me to fantasies it can never fulfill. It produces unexplainable, irrational behavior that later causes me puzzlement and shame. And, like lust and pride, money presents an arena of personal struggle that I will never "get over." It is a force with a personality. It is, in truth, a god, and Jesus called it that. [6]

The people and leaders of Nehemiah's day—in his absence—forgot that. They forgot that: *"Money can buy medicine, but not health. Money can buy a house, but not a home. Money can buy companionship, but not friends. Money can buy entertainment, but not happiness. Money*

*can buy food, but not an appetite. Money can buy a bed,
but not sleep. Money can buy a crucifix, but not a Savior.
Money can buy the good life, but not eternal life.* " [7]

We must never forget that because if we do, we will discover
that in doing so spiritual growth is easily traded for economic
advantage.

When that happens, a decline in morality often lies in the
wings. . .as compromise replaces conviction.

The promise the people made back in chapter 10—the
agreement they signed—had affirmed that intermarriage would
not happen. Now they've broken their promise. And the situation is serious for at least two reasons. First of all, because the
children of these mixed marriages could not speak Hebrew. Hebrew was the language of the Scripture, and they could glean
nothing from God's Word. Secondly, they had joined hands
with the Ammonites who worshiped the god Molech by sacri-
ficing their children to him in the fire. The Moabites worshiped
the god Chemosh, to whom they also sacrificed their children.
And the people were toying with that kind of idolatry. The
sobering fact that grips our attention is that a single generation's
compromise could potentially undo the work of centuries.

We are not immune from the peril today. In a perceptive
book, *Will Evangelism Survive Its Own Popularity?*, a book
that is more relevant today than when it was published in 1980,
John Johnston writes:

> *Current evangelical popularity presents powerful pres-
> sures to compromise biblical values for the sake of social
> acceptance. Our degree of compromise has reached epi-
> demic proportions.* [8]

Nehemiah has flown back to Jerusalem, and he's stumbled
across one problem after another. Without hesitation, he rolls
up his sleeves, takes a deep breath, and wades into the battle
with solutions that were absolutely necessary.

The first solution focuses on the *courage of convictions.* Nehemiah's no weakling in the wrestling match of faith. To defend Jehovah, Nehemiah was willing to risk everything.

And I came to Jerusalem and learned about the evil that Eliashib had done for Tobiah, by preparing a room for him in the courts of the house of God. And it was very displeasing to me, so I threw all of Tobiah's household goods out of the room. Then I gave an order and they cleaned the rooms; and I returned there the utensils of the house of God with the grain offerings and the frankincense (13:7-9).

In *The Integrity Crisis*, Warren Wiersbe comments: *"The Christian whom God wants to bless and use in the present crisis must have the courage to be different and the conviction to keep going in the right direction, come what may."* [9]

That's Nehemiah. He understood integrity. With all the energy of his forceful personality and in deep, righteous indignation, he acted—personally throwing out of the temple chambers all the household furniture of Tobiah. He then gives orders for the rooms to be fumigated and returned to their original purpose. And that takes courage—the courage of a man whose convictions are firmly established in God's Word.

You could never convince me that Nehemiah folded his hands and said, "Tsk, tsk, this is such a shame. We must pray about what we should do with Tobiah's belongings." No! He opened the door and said, "Haul that stuff out of here!"

Integrity. . .commitment to what is right. . .anchored Nehemiah's courage. It put steel in his bones, iron in his blood. The word *fearless* would be an apt description of his actions. He was committed to practicing the truth. This gave him a clear understanding of the difference between right and wrong. It also gave him the capacity to take decisive action. After throwing Tobiah out, he reprimanded the nobles of Jerusalem for profaning the Sabbath, rebuked the officials for neglecting the house of God, and he commanded the Levites to purify themselves and guard the gates to keep the Sabbath holy (10:11-22).

Yes. Nehemiah tackles the Sabbath wheeler-dealers. The verb *rebuked* is extremely strong. It's a red-face and white-knuckle verb. It means *"to contend with someone,"* and comes from a root that describes a noisy quarrel. Nehemiah let them have it for turning what was sacred into something common. But he went even further. Nehemiah ordered the heavy gates of the city closed during the Sabbath, and then he posted some of his private servants there to make sure they stayed closed and no one attempted to smuggle anything inside. Nehemiah's message was loud and clear: *"Knock it off, men. This is the end of the line."* When the guys in business suits didn't give up—they set up shop outside the city, hoping to draw business uptown a bit—Nehemiah didn't sit idly by. He warned them that he'd use force on them. "If you do this again, I will use force against you" (13:21).

Courage of conviction.

Some will say, "Couldn't this matter have been handled more diplomatically, more gently?" One commentator answers that question:

> *Doubtless we could debate the [method]. Yet in Christian work our cowardice in avoiding unpleasantness is currently doing more damage than any damage from [harshness] on the part of Christian leaders. . . .The Church has become flabby, old womanish, inept, unwilling to act. Discipline should be reconciliatory and loving, but it should take place. And on the whole it does not. . . .*[10]

Nehemiah saw the problem, recognized its evil, and stood to defend—not himself or his previous actions—but his God. His courage, firmness, and willingness to face the situation and act reveal a man of uncompromising conviction and personal courage.

Hugh Latimer was much like Nehemiah. He was one of the leaders of the English Reformation during the early 1500s. He was called in to preach before King Henry VIII; and as he preached, he offended Henry with his boldness. So he was called back the next week to preach before Henry and was warned that he had better not offend the King. So Hugh Latimer read his Scripture, he prayed, and then he preached exactly the same sermon again, only with more force. This was a man like Nehemiah! Would that we had more men like them today!

Because Nehemiah came with the courage of his convictions and in the power of God's Word, he was able to *reestablish some sagging priorities.* We saw the problem earlier. . .the focus of the temple had changed. . .people were not giving properly. So Nehemiah goes after the city officials (13:11-13). They should have addressed this problem a long time ago. It was part of their job. Apparently he got through to them because they set about encouraging the people to start giving again, and the people responded. Under Nehemiah's direction the priests and Levites resumed their former duties—the leading of worship and spiritual instruction. Spiritual priorities were reestablished.

Nehemiah's actions are remarkable when you consider that he stood to gain nothing personally from what he did. If anybody should have been interested enough to act, it should have been the high priest, Eliashib. The temple was his turf, his responsibility, and its proper operation would have been credited to him. Nehemiah gained no personal benefit by reproving greed and selfishness and reestablishing priorities.

So why'd he do it if he wasn't going to get anything out of it?

Because Nehemiah's priorities were God's priorities whether they were popular or unpopular, whether they would be to his personal advantage or not.

Does that describe us? John Chervokas, in his book, *How to Keep God Alive from 9 to 5,* puts this in terms we can understand:

—Maybe we work in a firm whose products are advertised in one of our country's sleaze magazines, those that demean women and our traditional values. How about starting an in-company campaign to get our company to pull the advertising out of the magazine?

—We work in the Purchasing Department and are constantly being taken to lunch, the theater, the ball game by a certain supplier. Now a mini-TV set from the supplier is delivered to our office. We grit our teeth, rewrap the set and send it back with a note, *"No more. . .no more."*

—We see a worker having the skids greased under his career by the company. Rather than shunning this person we go out of our way to befriend him and learn what's wrong in his job life or his home life that we might be able to correct.

—We're confronted, once again, by that colleague of ours who feels compelled to tell us of his latest sexual escapade while off on a business trip. He speaks of his most recent sexual adventure as proudly as he does of his wife and three kids. Rather than listen in leering interest to this guy one more time we screw up our courage and say to him, "You know, Mike, you're a jerk and let me tell you why. . . ." [11]

That's courage. That's taking a stand for God and His standards—even if it offends the crowd. When Nehemiah flew back into town. . .people knew it. He offered them a model of courage. . .of convictions. . .the reestablishment of priorities.

Finally, he gave them *decisive decisions.* We see that specifically when he deals with the problem of compromise in mixed marriages.

So I contended with them and cursed them and struck some

*of them and pulled out their hair, and made them swear by
God, "You shall not give your daughters to their sons, nor
take of their daughters for your sons or for yourselves"
(13:25).*

Nehemiah records his reactions to the problem. This man
was willing to call sin sin. He would tolerate *no* compromise of
God's standards.

These kinds of actions, to the Hebrew mind, were designed
to show anger, to express an insult, and to mark someone off to
scorn. That's how Nehemiah responded. And to follow it up he
made the people promise never to let it happen again.

To reinforce the point he drops into history and lifts out their
King Solomon as exhibit one. Everyone would have known the
story. Then to drive his point home, Nehemiah thunders,

*"Did not Solomon king of Israel sin regarding these
things? Yet among the many nations there was no king like
him, and he was loved by his God, and God made him king
over all Israel; nevertheless the foreign women caused
even him to sin. Do we then hear about you that you have
committed all this great evil by acting unfaithfully against
our God by marrying foreign women?" (13:26-27).*

Solomon was Israel's outstanding king in terms of wealth
and political achievements. He reigned 40 years. He built the
magnificent temple and an even more splendid palace for
himself. His fame spread to the extent that the Queen of Sheba
in southwestern Arabia traveled 1400 miles to test his fabled
wisdom. He held international prestige. . .but, he insisted on
defying God, on marrying unbelieving wives. . .and they led
him into sin. He did not pass go. . .he did not collect $200.
Solomon's reign began in humility as he asked the Lord to grant
him wisdom (II Chronicles 1:7-10; 6:14-42). Yet, in later years
he worshiped the god of the Moabites, Chemosh, and even built
an altar for it on the Mount of Olives.

Nehemiah's response to this peoples' disobedience was drastic and it was decisive. Notice that nowhere does he delegate the decision to act. Nowhere does he hold a board or committee meeting to look into these matters. He knows how to assess a situation, and he knew how to make decisions and act on those decisions. Nehemiah didn't care if it was the popular thing to do. He knew that he ran the serious risk of being misunderstood and that many would respond negatively. But that is the risk we take when we are prepared to respond to matters of disobedience.

It's the risk Nehemiah was prepared to take because his heartbeat was the spiritual revival of his people, and he was prepared to go the limit for it to happen. Are we?

Warren Wiersbe accurately describes Nehemiah when he says, *"That is the kind of leader we really need today. He has the courage to face problems honestly, the wisdom to understand them, the strength to do something about them and the faith to trust God to do the rest. He isn't afraid of losing friends or making enemies. He can't be intimidated by threats or bought with bribes. He is God's man and he isn't for sale."* [12]

The thousands of fans at Kezar Stadium knew all about Jimmy Brown. He was the All-Pro running back for the Cleveland Browns as they played the San Francisco '49ers in that 1957 game.

None of the fans knew about the ten-year-old boy who never saw the game even though he was in the stadium. He waited until the gate guard left after the third quarter and sneaked into the entrance of the players' tunnel. The lad was tall and skinny, the victim of ghetto poverty which had left him malnourished and crippled. He walked with the aid of steel splints.

When the game ended, the boy virtually blocked the tunnel until Brown came by and signed an autograph for him. But the boy wasn't satisfied with a signature. He pulled Brown's jersey and said, *"Mr. Brown, I have your picture on my wall. My family can't afford a TV set but I watch you on the neighbor's set every chance I get. I know what your records are and I think you're the greatest. You're my idol."*

Brown graciously thanked his young admirer and turned toward the locker room, but the boy wouldn't let go until he said one more thing. *"Mr. Brown, one day I'm going to break every one of your records!"*

The sincerity and conviction struck Brown. He asked, "What's your name, son?"

"Orenthal James, sir. But my friends call me O. J."

Sixteen years later, O. J. Simpson did what he promised, breaking Brown's single season rushing record and becoming the first NFL player to gain more than 2,000 yards rushing in one year. [13]

Having watched the game, Nehemiah's game, I want to run into the players' tunnel and wait for Nehemiah to pass by. I want to grab his sweaty, dirty jersey and tell him he's the greatest and that I'd like to run as he has run—only better...with God's help.

He was a hero but he was just an ordinary man willing to be used in extraordinary ways by God. A man of conviction, of courage, someone willing to make a difference.

God uses ordinary heroes. How are the walls of your life?

FOOTNOTES:

[1]Paul Aurandt, *More of Paul Harvey's The Rest of the Story,* (Bantam Books, New York, NY, 1980), pp. 134-135. Used with permission.

[2]Aleksander Solzhenitsyn, *East and West,* (Harper and Row, New York, NY, 1980), p. 45.

[3]Derek Kidner, *Ezra & Nehemiah,* (InterVarsity Press, Downer's Grove, IL, 1979), p. 129.

[4]Charles R. Swindoll, *Hand Me Another Brick,* (Thomas Nelson Publishers, Nashville, TN, 1978), pp. 192-193. Used with permission.

[5]Robert D. Foster, *The Challenge,* (Newsletter published by Robert Foster, Colorado Springs, CO, Dec. 1, 1988).

[6]Phillip Yancey, "Learning to Live With Money," *Christianity Today,* Dec. 14, 1984, p. 35.

[7]Charles R. Swindoll, *Strengthening Your Grip*, (Word, Inc., Dallas, TX, 1982), p. 85. Used with permission.

[8]John Johnston, *Will Evangelism Survive its Own Popularity?,* (Zondervan Corporation, Grand Rapids, MI, 1980), pp. 2, 13.

[9]Warren W. Wiersbe, *The Integrity Crisis,* (Oliver Nelson Books, Nashville, TN, 1988), p. 128.

[10]John White, *Excellence in Leadership,* (InterVarsity Press, Downer's Grove, IL, 1986), pp. 123-124.

[11]John V. Chervokas, *How To Keep God Alive from 9 to 5,* (Doubleday Books, Garden City, NY, 1986), pp. 76-77. Used with permission.

[12]Warren W. Wiersbe, Ibid., pp. 73-74.

[13]Leith C. Anderson, *Making Things Happen,* (Victor Books, Wheaton, IL, 1987), pp. 32-33.